SEXY
~*MAGNETIC*~
YOU

BY VANESSA SMITH

Cover Photo Credit:
ERIC DEBRIS/ www.kustomdebris.com
Cover illustration by Agsandrew
Extended License granted for use.

Interior illustrations by Vanessa Smith

Special thanks to Eric Helms, Adelyn Botto,
Mary Elizabeth and Mia Dean for helping me
with the editing process. Truly you have all
been the cat's meow and I am forever grateful,
thank you!

I also want to share my deepest gratitude for
my *fantastic* family and friends for all the love
and support and for being the inspiration to
always raise the roof and celebrate this
beautiful life we share together.

CONTENTS:

DEDICATON

I dedicate this book to the wounds that we carry within us, those parts of ourselves that have been cast away in frozen silent judgment, secretly holding us back from receiving the fulfillment we deserve. I dedicate this book to the healing of these wounds so that we may be whole, honoring ourselves with truth so we can heal those parts once and for all through the light of unconditional love.

INTRODUCTION

This book is for those who are ready for dynamic change.

All lasting change comes from within. You can chase happiness and run from pain but if you do not embrace the courage that's within you to face the truth of you, you will always be chasing and searching for what you cannot contain; if you don't know your truth and haven't yet honored your wounds with healing, nothing will truly fulfill you because you can't honor and fulfill the true you and your needs if you haven't yet looked within and embraced the whole of you.

This book explores the common misconceptions about love, empowerment and healing while shining a light on powerful tools we can utilize to help guide our way through our deeper realms with unconditional love. Exploring and healing our inner world is the key to empowering our choices so we can live our lives with crystal clear clarity and pure intention, powerfully creating happiness in our lives.

Sexy Magnetic You is within you just waiting to be
AWAKENED!

You are a GIFT and the more you focus on your own healing, the more you have to offer as you release limiting beliefs and conditioning, replacing them with irresistible happiness and peace.

Vanessa Smith is a Sexy Magnetic Musician, Hypnotherapist, NLP Practitioner and Demolition Coach who has been practicing the Art of Transformational Healing and Empowerment since the fall of 2006.

Vanessa has been working on her own healing since she was the age of 15 overcoming many deep and heavy challenges.

As she searched for healing, the path of Hypnotherapy and the Healing Arts paved the way for her inner clarity so she could own her gifts and share them unashamedly.

Vanessa has dedicated her life to Transformational Healing by utilizing the tools within her own life and helping her incredible clients to facilitate empowerment by overcoming obstacles; healing their wounds by honoring them and their wisdom within, bathing their wounds in the most powerful force of all, unconditional love.

Vanessa has made it her mission to share this empowerment with the rest of the world. As we heal ourselves we heal the world around us. The effects of honoring our own healing process by facing ourselves with truth and unconditional love creates quantum activators that create very real and powerful change as we release the chains that bind us, owning our strength to shape this world beyond our own amazement.

So... Let's BEGIN>>>

CHAPTER 1
Commit to your Inner Soul Mate
& BECOME MAGNETIC LOVE

I know what some of you are thinking! Commit to my what? I don't even know if I believe in Soul Mates yet you're telling me there's one within me?

Yes, that's just it! Most of us are longing and searching for some spectacular love from outside of ourselves to come rushing in and make everything alright. We long to be acknowledged and seen, to be the shiny treasure of someone else's life, yet we forget to acknowledge and see ourselves as the shiny treasure of our own lives. How will anyone be able to see the beauty within us if we ourselves have not yet embraced it? It's like attempting to sell a product that we haven't even tried! We know nothing of its true value, yet wonder why we can't seem to sell the damn thing!

The number one reason many of us can't comprehend the idea of soul mates, especially an inner soul mate, is because we haven't begun the journey within to know our own inner lover, our twin flame... the essence that we long to share with that special someone, someday... when everything is perfect.

We're all waiting for Prince Charming or Wonder Woman to come along and discover the awesomeness we're hiding within us and gallop us off into the "happily ever after" Sunset.

The problem with this scenario is that we put on a pretty face and a show for our potential suitors..."Ta-DA!!! Here I am! Rock me like a Hurricane!"

This is all well and wonderful and endorphin releasing ... until our deeper and truer Self tires of maintaining false perfection, and begins to question this attraction, this "love," this attention.

A significant obstacle in our path to love is that we may not truly believe that we deserve someone who sticks with us once our true colors overshadow the "perfect" phase.

Subconsciously we create a false foundation expecting it to crumble, so we aren't too surprised when it doesn't work out. In all honesty who's to say if we really wanted it to work out in the first place?

The secret is until we truly believe that we are unashamedly deserving of the truest, bluest, most romantic love, we will sabotage it in sneaky, "I'm the victim" ways. We do this to uphold underlying beliefs that we do NOT deserve love and are safer alone.

We feel less vulnerable if we can hide these unflattering beliefs, all the while being an expert on why relationships don't work.

In a sense, we have become a society of, "A.D.D. Love," always on the lookout for a shinier object when the illusion of perfection fades. But in most cases it's our own imperfections that come to light. If we don't embrace and love those parts of ourselves unconditionally, we'll manifest temporary role-fulfilling relationships missing out on the sweetest alchemical honey from within.

So that's the hurdle one has to make. Does one choose to truly face the truth of one's self in love and life and dare to know the lover within and look at all their uncomfortable "imperfections"; or do they continue to keep it cool and play the game of role fulfillment?

I'll be your Princess Leia if you'll be my Han Solo
and vice versa as long as our true selves don't pipe in
we can make a great movie together about love... but
let's keep it to a normal feature length because I look
forward to seeing my name in the end credits where
we both move on to our next roles and coming
attractions.

Not that marriage and monogamy are the answers.
There are all sorts of lifestyle choices one can make,
but I will say there is so much more to be gained and
experienced when there is 100% truth and honesty
with one's self and 100% truth and honesty with the
other/s in whichever dance we choose.

In all fairness when I speak of role-fulfillment most of
us don't even realize we're putting on an act because
it's a conditioned and learned behavior we've taken
on from our role models and the media. How many
Hollywood movies truly capture the essence of love
that has grown past the glitz and glam?

I firmly believe that there is no mistake in this conditioning because when we are a society of fear and doubt afraid to break the roles we think we should be playing, we are a society that is easily manipulated and controlled.

Do you want to create empowering change in this world? Step into the transformational bounty of LOVE and open up to the endless possibilities around you to be the changes you seek- in a vibration of celebration, not fear.

And yes, there are still endless accounts of INCREDIBLE LOVE despite this ingrained role fulfillment behavior. True love is transformational and through love we learn, grow and move through the most challenging of times. When we finally break through the polite perfectionism and show the more insecure parts we've been holding back we can begin to grow and learn to accept ourselves and our partner's true being.

The truth and heart of the matter of why I'm writing this book is there is an endless sea of love that has barely been tapped into, and it is an incredible source of complete and total amazement. To only buy the shallow story of Hollywood love is to sell the soul of humanity short because it is our ability to love that makes humanity so truly outstanding. We have been misguided and cut off from our endless empowering source of Love for far too long.

Committing to loving ourselves through thick or thin and honoring our big picture sends the sweetest invitation for incredible magnetism to come our way. When we love the parts of ourselves we've abandoned, we become whole again which in turn helps us to truly begin to give and receive love and all its potential.

CHAPTER 2
COMMIT TO LOVE

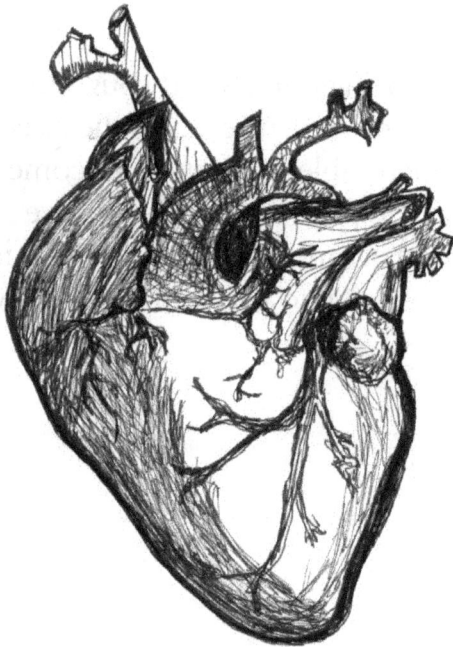

LOVE is a powerful tool for healing ourselves and this planet. The essential knowledge of love being an alchemical energetic system has been suppressed for hundreds of thousands of years. We have been taught as a society not to love. We have been trained on so many levels for war and separation that it's been incredibly hard to even believe in love let alone experience its transformational bounty.

We are echoing one giant broken heart after the other passing down one sorrow filled wound from one generation to the next. We are all carrying the weight of our ancestor's grief, shame, sorrow, guilt and regrets trying our best to make a piece of happiness and touch a little love in this lifetime through all the hustle and bustle of it all.

This travesty is exactly why it's beyond time to COMMIT TO LOVE! We have been broken for far too long, and now it's time the tidal wave of love's unstoppable ability to heal shines through the darkness and into the light of our hearts.

It is our sweetness that we haven't even begun to taste and not to know the infinite sea of love that flows within us is a robbery and a crime executed upon only those who deny love in all its transformational beauty.

Our fears and doubts block our connection to this bounty of love within us, keeping us in a dangerously comfortable place of living a surface life, numb to our own awe-inspiring amazement.

We are conditioned to wait for validation from an outside source before we can finally respect ourselves in the eyes of love; this is like waiting for permission to breathe.

~~~~We ARE love.~~~~

Just close your eyes and connect to that feeling within you when you think of that special someone you would move the world for; that feeling within you is love, and no one can give you that, they can inspire it and show you a new depth within you, but it lives in you! It is YOU!

Although we may be a society of A.D.D. Love and self-doubt, we are also a society that is filled with dreams, hopes, and ambitions. If you took the majority of any room and really took the time to connect with each individual, you'd see a SEA OF CONNECTION.

Although war has been programmed into our society, it is actually peace that is the natural order if we allow for true connection. It is my experience that, "truly" reaching out to our fellow human beings is more than well received at least 90% of the time!

If we are willing to open our eyes to our humanity, it will greet us with open arms and with deep gratitude for shining a light, our light, which is the true gift of humanity.

It is this kind of awareness that can create quantum shifts in our society. If we can begin at the micro levels of creating peace and happiness within ourselves we in turn spread that joy and ability to those around us.

Just like every drop in the sea creates the massive movement of the ocean, our waves are more powerful than we have been lead to believe.

It all begins within *EACH AND EVERY ONE OF US.* How is peace ever to exist if we are at war with ourselves? It's been said, and I'll say it again, if we want to end war, we must start by ending the wars within us and around us in our everyday lives.

Embracing the parts of ourselves that we cast off as unworthy or lesser is the first step to healing and accepting our differences- our strengths and weaknesses within ourselves, each other and our societies.

Our hearts create the highest frequencies that ignite the strongest electromagnetic and energetic vibrations in and around our physical bodies. This understanding has the power and MAGNITUDE to truly challenge the value systems we've been handed to carry as a society.

Our HEARTS carry the seed, the magic for transforming ourselves, our lives and our societies- to quite literally create heaven on Earth: this is our natural path when we are connected to the unstoppable force of LOVE.

This transformational energy is available with each heartbeat if we are willing to listen to its call, its wisdom, and embrace its transformational light!

We are a beautiful humanity who's been handed the lie of separation, war, and desperation, and it is up to us to choice to take our power back and create a beautiful world for ourselves and each other.

Exercise:

Go out and connect with your humanity! See what kind of magic you can ignite by simply being present and curious about how you can connect with your environment and lift the energetic vibration to one of connection and support. Sincerely connect with your fellow humanity and do so not just with the super shiny, attractive people but EVERYONE. Have FUN with this!

CHAPTER 3
In Judgment We
~ TRUST~

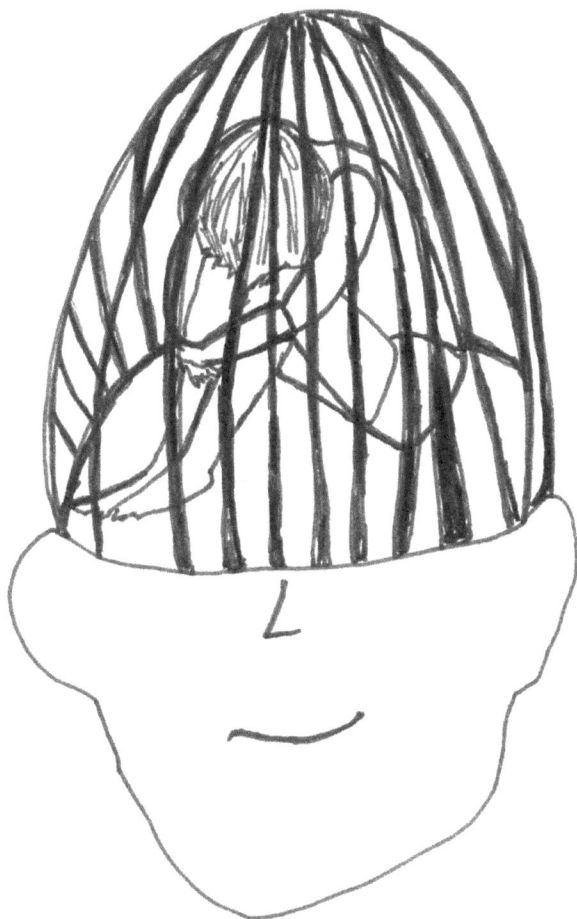

Our programmed educational systems teach us there is typically one correct answer that we must choose in order to be right; this conditions us to believe we should all want to be right because if we are not right then we must be wrong. If we are wrong and do not answer correctly, we will not move forward in life.

Bingo, we've found one of our major wounds. The very idea of being able to measure our intelligence and ability via one method as if one size fits all is a crime against our ~DIVINE DIVERSITY~ which is one of the gems within our ever changing incredibly talented humanity.

We are a powerful species multifaceted beyond belief yet we have barely tapped into the gift that we truly are and are meant to be.

We can NOT simply allow ourselves to all be lumped into one homogenized category within our intellect, abilities, talents and ways of experiencing our World; this is a degrading outdated system that keeps us in a judgmental thinking pattern.

When there is only one right the rest must be wrong. If you don't fit into this one method of learning or being than you are insufficient and insignificant; this is the beginning of judgment and the basis for WAR.

We grow from being innocent little beings filled with trust, wonder, and AWE to being taught our value on a measuring stick. As we grow we begin to self -inflict these debilitating self- judgments of comparison of how we are not right in all these different calculated measures.

If we are not right then we must be wrong. If we are wrong how are we ever going to move forward in life, love or anything else that we long for? This is why we wear an armor of perfectionism. After all it's what is expected of us if we are to succeed.

This conditioned rightness extends to our media teaching us how we should look, dress, what we should eat, desire and dream for ourselves; creating the measurements we should now judge ourselves against.

The scope of individuality within each and every one of us is so great that we can no longer sacrifice and punish ourselves by comparing ourselves constantly.

We are not robots, clones or cookie cutter perfect creatures here to sell each other short by being something other than our truest most unique identity which is our gift to share with one another.

We are ALL unique and one of a kind with something that no one else can bring to the table. We are uniquely attuned to who we are in our essence, our spirits, our souls and our intellect and in our unique abilities, talents and ways of learning and experiencing our worlds.

The only way to turn the judgment paradigm around is through the HEART of the matter. Going within and activating unconditional love heals all and embraces the darkest places of the soul reigniting its flame.

There is no place for judgment within unconditional love. When we judge ourselves, we end up putting parts of ourselves into little prisons, punishing ourselves for not being perfect. When we refuse to acknowledge these parts of ourselves, we banish them to the darkness, this is where stress, illness and dis~ease have the opportunity to take control.

If we were to treat our physical bodies like we do our internal selves, we would soon see the cost of this abuse.

Imagine judging your foot because it somehow seems less attractive than the other foot and then imagine attempting to walk while bandaging it up so tightly that the circulation is cut off because you don't want anyone else to see.

That wouldn't go too smoothly would it? In fact, it would make the situation worse but unlike the internal judgments we cast on ourselves we'd be forced to create harmony and accept our foot the way it is and be grateful for its extremely useful purpose or end up an amputee.

We must start to accept and love ourselves as a whole being with all of our strengths, weaknesses, and perfect imperfections if we are to heal.

We are electromagnetic beings, and our feelings create our reality faster than our thoughts. If we feel crummy, we cultivate a crummy environment for crummy situations to come join and validate our crummy self -pity party.

Excitingly the same is true for feeling happy, confident and successful.

We are Magnets!

The sooner we embrace responsibility for our happiness the sooner we can walk in step with our heart's deepest desires.

If we feel we deserve something, it manifests. Like attracts like energy both positively and negatively. Journeying to our depths and activating love from within and opening ourselves to embracing every aspect of our own perfect imperfections is a chance to experience the treasure of love's transformational compassion, and it's endless creative ability to ignite and inspire expansive growth.

When we refuse to love ourselves unconditionally we end up in a cage of shame and judgment; stunting our growth and ability to see the hidden blessings of alchemy waiting to be found in the disguise of discomfort or imperfection.

There is a positive intention to most negatives. We can find these by looking into the secondary gain of the ailment. Secondary gain is the positive that is gained from the struggle.

When we look into this honestly and with non-judgment, we can get to the root and find a positive way to fulfill the positive intention thus no longer needing the negative to fulfill the positive.

The awareness and understanding that comes in through this process tends to transform most issues instantaneously especially if addressed at the roots of our mind, the subconscious.

Loving ourselves unconditionally and embracing our truth allows us to no longer need a mask of perfectionism to hide behind because our own unique beauty is far greater than anything else we could dream of trying to fit into.

We are the only container for our souls in this lifetime and as we honor ourselves and our unique beauty and processes we can begin to blossom in our gifts and share our treasure with the world.

Exercise:
How, where and why do you judge yourself?

How do you respond to this judgment?

How do you hold that judgment?

If you held it in your body, where would it be? How can you acknowledge and heal this? Where do you judge others the most?

Write a list and explore this. These are areas you too need to do some work because they are merely a reflection of your own dissatisfaction you carry within yourself.

Please be kind and honest with yourself. There is no need to add additional judgments on top of your judgments for having these judgments!

Come from your heart and be honest and open to healing these pockets of judgment and appreciate them for their pivotal lesson.

Welcome the darkness with the light, both are here to teach and awaken us to our strengths.

CHAPTER 4
If We Don't HEAL IT, We DEAL IT!

We are a society conditioned to be comfort seekers. Why look at uncomfortable truths or take action towards a challenging goal or desire when there are so many comforting distractions available to us constantly.

We can choose to mask our way through life and dance on the surface and for many this is all that is desired; this is an available choice just like everything because if we get down to it, everything is a CHOICE.

If there's a desire to heal and move beyond the surface the only way is through the difficulty or challenge not two-stepping around it.

There's also a certain amount of pride that can keep us stuck like nothing else. We are proud creatures, and we have much to be proud about, but this image of strength can be incredibly stifling. I say this being one of the many warriors out there who has had to survive a LOT! One has to grow a thick skin to survive in this sometimes challenging and abusive world.

We can get stuck in these walls of strength looking like the ROCK of confidence all the while actually coasting on automatic pilot with the image of strength yet forgetting to open to our true strength that is found in the value of our vulnerability to our inner truths.

True strength takes the time to look at the places we feel lesser or weak. Like a physical trainer would point out if we need to strengthen our legs if we held all of our strength mostly in our upper body; it is the same within our mental, emotional and spiritual bodies.

We must stop being so proud of these walls we hold as strength and open to our true strength by honoring our weaker sides and the lessons they have for us to EXPLORE!

Just like a seed planted and rooted in darkness/manure (=shit) for what might feel like an eternity to a seedling before it bursts through the surface and tastes the sweetness of the Sun; it is through this challenge or difficulty that we truly GROW.

It is through the darkness that we find the light. The night becomes the day and the day becomes the night both equally important and vitally necessary for ultimate balance and discovery.

"The only thing we have to fear is FEAR itself."
~Franklin D. Roosevelt

Yup! Fear is such a road block. We tend to take the long route over and over again just to avoid facing, "IT" but in the end facing, "IT" is the fastest way to get where we truly want to be.

One of my favorite quotes is,
"Fear is EXCITEMENT without the breath!"
~Fritz Perls

Choosing to breathe into the pain, difficulty and/or fear is the most powerful step we can take to empower ourselves and can quite literally shift things into amazement by creating a new awareness from the wisdom of the challenge.

Some of the most incredibly empowering things in life are, in most cases, the SIMPLEST!

This is good news for most but for us proud folks we aren't always ready to accept this blessing. The beautiful truth of the matter is this, we have a choice. We can make it as challenging or as simple as we'd like; this is our oxygen and we can choose how we want to use it!

So, the way out is through and it's exactly how it sounds. That uncomfortable thing you are ignoring; you know what I'm talking about! If you don't know, ask yourself, if I did know... what is it?
Now walk towards it? Yes, this is the beginning of EMPOWERMENT.

We are taught to run and hide. All this does is keep us in the dark from realizing that we are actually in heaven if we dare to truly open our eyes and hearts to the matter at hand through the eyes of self-acceptance and unconditional love.

It is my belief that we all came here with a clear intention of what we want to heal within our humanity and signed up to take on whatever experience within this lifetime that will best facilitate this healing.

Our struggles and challenges are what we came here to heal and learn. We are ALL healers. Many people disagree with the label/title healer but if we think about it, if we have an immune system we are all HEALERS because WE HEAL, the healing is within us.

When we heal ourselves, we inspire our humanity to do the same.

It is THROUGH the difficulty that we are able to learn, grow and transform. Like the skin of a snake shedding into complete renewal, it is by honoring and releasing our tears and fears that help us to shed that which no longer serves us.

IF WE DON'T HEAL IT, WE DEAL IT!

When we choose to heal we are choosing to end the line of abuse and thus sending quantum healing in all directions.

When we choose to HEAL whatever it is, we are not saying that we agree with what happened. We are simply choosing to refuse to continue the abuse by allowing its abusive energy to remain awake within us but instead choosing to heal it by bringing the situation to peace and empowerment instead.

When we heal our wounds we are healing the past, present and healing the future from having to carry what we would have otherwise passed down the line unconsciously subconsciously.

We cannot let something go if we are unwilling to face, "IT". When we face our demons, they transform beautifully into Angels or whatever symbolism translates best for you.

If we are willing to learn from the challenges and discomfort, we can then grow from the wisdom they are here to bestow upon us. These challenges are here as our teachers and guides to help us to embrace our greater strengths and abilities to heal and become more fully aware of who we truly are.

As we learn to honor ourselves, we transform beyond the difficulty into grace.

Transformational healing naturally begins its process quite effortlessly simply by the sheer act of acknowledging the fear, challenge or difficulty.

Everything has a purpose, and if we are willing to look for it, we will always find its higher purpose for us in store.

CHAPTER 5
The Heart BREAKS!

We've all been there. When we share the vulnerable beauty of love's endless depth with our trust intact while opening ourselves and sharing that invaluable vulnerability with the ones we love; when things go sour, and the sweetness turns cold, we are left shattered to pick up the pieces, overexposed, raw and DEEP in it.

The cold isolation tempts us to cover ourselves with armor preparing for battle as we get into a protective stance to block ourselves from feeling like the idiot we must be for believing in the naivety of love. We don a protective encasing to shield us from allowing this vulnerable exposure anytime soon or possibly ever again.

Unfortunately, this creates a very real separation within ourselves as we cast the ignorant lover we judge ourselves to be deep into the dungeon for allowing this depth of sorrow to take place in our hearts and our lives; all the while creating a wall of intellectual agreements about love and how to avoid this mockery from ever taking place again.

Healing the wounds of a broken heart is a very challenging process that can be incredibly consuming. Our hearts can be broken from a number of situations not just romantic but especially romantic. Doing our best we attempt to walk our daily lives with an open wound trying to mask it and/or perhaps even lashing out at the world around us in one way or another overly sensitive from the deep thorn in our hearts.

When we are drunk from the pain of heartbreak, it's easy to grow callous and fill ourselves with anger, hurt, blame and unmistakable shame; this is where we must learn the power of choice.

We must consciously and subconsciously choose to be the heart that is willing to BREAK and to take the time to HEAL and explore the valuable vulnerability of our heart's sorrows and lessons. We must allow ourselves to grow STRONGER in our ability to love instead of close ourselves off from the most transformational energy in the world just so we won't have to taste the depths of sorrow our broken heart is pulsating.

There is one major decision that needs to be made in order to begin the process of healing.

We must choose to take responsibility for our sorrow and choose to cast off the role of victim. If we want to be a victim, THAT IS ALL WE WILL EVER BE.

Not to be insensitive to the intensity but the sooner one chooses to take responsibility for the devastation the sooner one can step back into their power and grow stronger in their ability to love instead of getting savvier with their protective anger.

I know this because I am in the challenge of heartbreak right now as I'm writing this. As enlightened or evolved as we may feel we are, when it comes to romantic love, we are all faced with a constant learning curve of vulnerability.

I've been safe for a while but have recently opened to touch the very expansive feelings of love in a highly unexpected and challenging way but if I'm honest with myself, I could see the danger right in front of me but chose to dive in anyway.

It is so easy to blame the other person for not behaving in an agreeable way but really it is my own inner feelings that I ignored that allowed me to be caught in this dangerous space in the first place.

We teach people how to treat us in very unconscious ways and until we see this and recognize this we will continue to relearn the same lessons until we own our creation of the situation.

So how do we heal a broken heart?

My answer is LOVE. I went through the gamut of very deep stormy emotions for over a month and went through everything I've already mentioned and some. I was bitter, tempted to become and stay jaded, full of blame and in a lot of pain. I was sinking my energy into this emotional abyss and having a super crummy month in all aspects because of it.

I felt so embarrassed and ashamed being in the process of writing this book and feeling like the worst example of the truest intentions I have for writing this.

But as the dust began to settle and I began to own the situation; I soon realized this is exactly what I needed to be going through for this book to have its truest ground. I needed to be IN it to truly touch the heart, my heart of the matter and address the intensity of the depths of sorrow and to speak from personal experience by living these words I write to you; this is the blessing in disguise or as I like to call it the diamonds in the bullshit.

Diamonds in the bullshit- is a powerhouse approach to life. It's all about making the decision to use all challenges for good not evil and always to look for the treasure and the hidden gems of the situation. It all boils down to perspective and taking the reins to be the creator of your life instead of a victim.

There are no mistakes in life. When we choose to take ownership for our ups and downs and own the understanding that for some reason and in some way this is for my greater good and not my demise at all; all hardships truly can become blessings in disguise.

So how do we reclaim ourselves from the place of being shattered sinking into an emotional abyss?

As I said earlier, we need to step out of the victim vibration as soon as possible!

I don't mean to say that we should ignore our wounds and invalidate them in any way, on the contrary, I say follow the path of your sorrow; the feeling of lack, mistrust, blame, abuse, betrayal or rejection... whatever it may be and rather than blaming and shaming ourselves and the others truly take a good LOOK at it instead.

For me, it was the realization that I knowingly opened myself up to a situation that was booby-trapped from the get-go; this is where some active self-discovery can help me to see why I am manifesting these lessons and what purpose they serve.

So here I am, with the realization that somewhere within me, I somehow don't believe I deserve my truest hearts desires if I'm not willing to create a strong, clear foundation to see that fundamental needs are met but instead walking right into a booby-trap just because the attraction was so great, like a moth to the flame.

This may be a painful and somewhat embarrassing realization but this is where if I take the time to do my own personal work I can open up to creating and manifesting an overflowing abundance of love, strength and trust leaving the booby-trapped experiences in the past with nothing but gratitude for the lessons and transformation they have brought me.

So yes, LOVE is the answer...
- To love myself even though I let myself walk into a booby-trapped scene. I chose to love myself even though I felt rejected and used.

I chose to BE the open arms I needed to heal from these feelings. I had to look myself in the mirror and say, "Vanessa, I love you even though you are in this pain. Even though you feel anger, I love you for your willingness to grow beyond the anger and pain. I love you for seeing this is your own doing and choosing to own it and be responsible for it. I love you, Vanessa, even if there is a part of you that feels you don't deserve the truest love, I still unconditionally love that part of YOU."

Taking this time to love myself and to take ownership was essential for transforming the intensity into productive clarity.

One of the pivotal steps I took was taking the time to be outside and connect with the amazing healing qualities of our Mother Earth. I would sit peacefully connecting to my breath and asking for nature's guidance in healing this difficulty. The wisdom came in to quite literally take my power back by calling all parts of myself that belong to me to come back to me where they belong.

I'd sit with the Earth and imagine I was a GIANT MAGNET, calling all parts of myself that I needed to regain my strength; calling them home to my place of strength and balance and as I did I could clearly see the role of victim no longer fitting me.

I could feel myself choosing to open my heart instead of close it. I chose to embrace everyone involved in the light of love and to honor them with love, not anger. I found myself choosing to agree to look at the pain as my teacher instead of running away from it. I chose to be willing to BE the love I needed instead of feeling abandoned by it. I chose to love myself and my attraction both unconditionally. I chose to look at it all as a blessing instead of a curse as I looked for ways to grow from the challenge.

I chose to trust that this was all part of a brilliant plan for my greatest good. I chose to release my attraction from having to play the role that obviously wasn't meant in this space and time. I chose to see if I could shift my feelings of a crushed dream into compassion for his truth. I chose to see if I could transform the romantic love vibration I was feeling that wasn't returned to finding a path that we could meet on that served us both in truth.

All of this is easier said than done... I KNOW! But it is so much more rewarding, transformational and empowering than sticking to the old ways of victim role-playing.

The truth is it takes time to do the personal work but once you've done it, you've won it! You can then look at these painful moments with gratitude for showing you your inner strength, beauty, and wisdom.

Healing a broken heart comes in many phases and layers. The first step is to embrace the myriad emotions and simply being IN it. If we have a heart, it is going to BREAK from one experience or the next, and it's a natural cycle that is meant to bring us deeper into our understanding of our expansive ability to heal and GROW in strength, beauty, love and truth.

Unless we want to short change ourselves and the expansive growth we have coming to us; there truly are no shortcuts. We've got to truly feel our emotions and learn to acknowledge, honor, heal and release them. Once we've begun to allow ourselves to feel and acknowledge them by letting the tears, anger and pain have their say, its then time to accept the situation. To say yes to the pain, anger and challenge instead of burying it down deep and encasing ourselves in armor or drowning it in an addiction of some sort, all of which is detrimental to our health and well-being.

Hollywood likes to glamorize pain with addictions or to don a callous character, but all these methods accomplish is to prolong and cultivate more pain and sorrow all the while hiding us in the shadows from our own light.

When we say yes to the pain and acknowledge it, this is when we can begin to heal it. Our emotions are like children who just need to be heard and to have their vulnerable feelings validated and to cry and shed a tear so the emotion can be honored and then released because it's served its' purpose. We are not the robots we have been programmed to be.

When we dare to delve into the darker realms of emotion armed with unconditional love, ready to embrace the most unlovable parts of ourselves; we set our wounded beauty previously masked as a monster free.

It is our light we've grown shy as a humanity to shine. We hold dark expectations as medals to our trails of war and despair proving we aren't weak dreamers here to be fooled by loves childish and dreamy ideals.

We are the creators of our lives, and it is imperative that we wake up to this because it's the KEY to empowering our lives and our world!

Healing the roots of these feelings of pain will always lead us to empowered clarity. When we choose to walk towards the discomfort and listen to its words, its pain, its lesson for being in our lives; this is the fastest way to turn the entire challenge around into a GIANT blessing.

We are so used to running away by acting strong and brave, mistaking this for strength. True strength is in the vulnerability. When we expose ourselves and allow the raw emotions to breathe, we can find our ground in clarity.

We can choose to embrace our challenges by using them as tools for empowerment; choosing to see its' purpose which is actually here to help us in ways we simply can't always see right away.

As always... it comes down to TRUST.
___I_____   _____TRUST_____
I will make it to the other side of uncertainty.

Choosing to be the heart that is willing to break means choosing to believe that no matter what happens we will be stronger for it all the while saying yes to love and all its expansive transformational beauty.

Exercise:

Even though I _____, I love myself
unconditionally.

Even though I_____, I deeply love and
accept myself.

Even though I _____, I now choose to see
the lesson it's here to teach me.

Even though _____, I now choose to
release the victim role and take ownership of the
situation.

Even though I/they _____
I forgive myself/them/ us for taking this on.

I accept this challenge as my teacher, thank you for
teaching me_____.

I love and accept myself. I was doing the best I could
and now I have learned and grown from this
experience and choice to see it in an empowered light.

CHAPTER 6
ForGIVE!

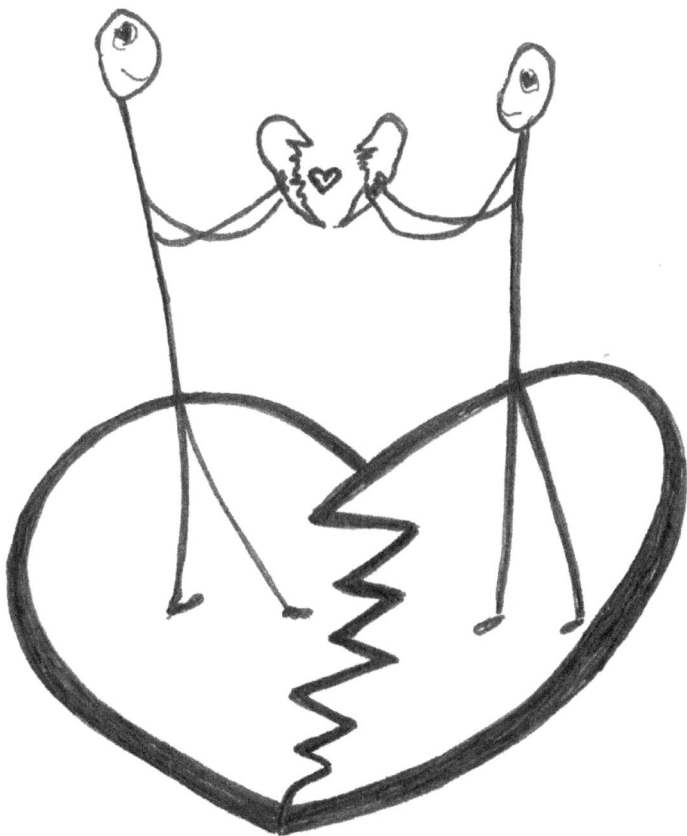

OH, BOY... Do *what* now?

Forgiving can be difficult, especially when we've allowed ourselves to believe that a part of our personality has become one with the anger and resentment. We carry said hardships as if they are now a part of our being.

Yes, this happens, more often than not and is a big part of the victim game but again it's an ingrained conditioned response, so there's no need to judge it. Simply noticing it for the first time can be quite exciting as it frees us up to create more empowering and imaginative versions of ourselves instead of just wearing the jaded wounded, "I'm right because I was wronged!" heavy judgmental vibe.

Sadly we hear the sweet romantic violin playing the poor us victim tune that unfortunately is pure quicksand. Some people end up addicted to this and get stuck with the victim violin for a lifetime. They assume it's all they have when in fact there is always a choice of empowerment for the taking.

It's in forgiving and consciously deciding to end the energy leakage of the blame game by deciding to choose to learn from the experience and move on instead of being the-"I'm in the right!" victim zone.

When we consciously choose to forGIVE, we give ourselves our power back because we are no longer leaking our energy and sinking it into anger, resentment or blame. We can instead GIVE ourselves constructive feedback and productively move forward in the direction of our choosing.

There is ALWAYS an empowered choice for the choosing; it's all in the choices we make.

Again, if we want to be a victim... best of luck because we are going to need all the luck in the universe to get our magnetism to a shiny place of magnetizing our true desires because the victim role will only attract more victim role playing that is a one-way ticket to Bummerville.

The only way I know this to be true is because I've spent a good deal of my life in the victim zone. I'll tell you from experience, never looking back is the best option.

When we notice we are playing a victim, it's in our best interest to take note and get busy on making clear and intention based chooses to create what we truly want.

Committing to being the only one accountable for our success AND our failure is an incredible path to happiness as well as a powerful path to becoming an excellent leader as well; good for us and good for those around us! When I speak of leadership, I speak of those who inspire and serve their fellow humanity, not those who control and manipulate. True leadership inspires others to see and embrace their highest potential so that they can then lead their own path of gifts to share unashamedly.

We are not our wounds! We are healers of the wound. Heroes and Heroines heal and transform the wounds and become *A WAKENED* because of it.

Here's the thing, abuse follows abuse, follows abuse. IF WE DON'T HEAL IT, WE DEAL IT and so on and so on.

Want to change the world?

End the line of abuse by healing it within yourself and forGIVING those who brought it onto you, giving them a chance to start anew. Forgiveness and healing are quantum activators that extend their abilities to transform in all directions....

~ ~ ~ ~ ~ ~ ~ ~Past, Present and Future~ ~ ~ ~ ~ ~

There is no need for a time machine when you empower the present moment with transformational healing and complete and total forgiveness. Just WOW, is all I have to say about that!

When looking back at an abusive scene we can take the pain of yesterday and defuse its past crippling hold by adjusting the negative imprint we took on from the experience and choose to see it as a part of our story but not the defining part of who we are and how we choose to live our lives.

When we truly forgive we are reclaiming our energy that would otherwise be zapping our lives from finding fulfillment in those avenues we're still holding the toxins of hatred, blame and anger in. These are heavy emotions that when fueled can rob one of happiness for years if not a lifetime if not properly faced, embraced and released into the arms of forgiveness.

And when we speak of forgiveness, we must grant ourselves that very same forgiveness.

- Forgiveness for not being perfect.
- Forgiveness for magnetizing such intense challenges into our lives.

- Forgiveness for mistreating ourselves and others.

- Forgiveness for judging ourselves and others.

- Forgiveness for misunderstandings that lead to so much pain and suffering.

There is so much room and need for forgiveness to heal the karma of our humanity that it could take decades of focusing on forgiveness alone, to free us from our past sins for lack of a better word.

It's so important to learn to let go and forgive the pain from the past and forgive its past hold and free ourselves from the shackles of blame so we can create a new path cleared from the encapsulation of pain and negativity the past was dressed in.

Yesterday or yesteryear do not define our today and our tomorrow... **we do!**

I am a survivor of rape among many other forms of abuse.
Can I forgive my abusers?
Yes.

Not to say that this task is easy breezy in any way; it can be a very long road to get here but such a worthy place to get to; this is a possibility I wish to offer to those who have been through the unmentionable.

Not that I condone what happened to me or wish for anyone to have to go through that kind of devastation and violation or get away with that kind of devastation and violation.

I simply choose to be the healer of that abuse. To end the line of abuse so no one has to suffer the depths of sorrow because of my lack of healing. Abuse follows abuse follows abuse... if we don't HEAL it, we deal it.

THE ABUSE STOPS HERE!

As I heal these wounds that have taken a good deal of my life, I rinse the sorrow of the ingrained messages of unworthiness my abusers installed in me down the drain, never to return because I am unwilling to allow those violations to rob me of my spirit, my life, my passion, my heart, my desire to heal and to choose to be truly free from the past.

I choose to do the personal work it takes to walk a path that is new and free for me to choose my choices for myself, my life, my happiness and my FULFILLMENT!

Forgiveness is not forgetting or agreeing with whatever abuse or wrong -doing that may have taken place.

Forgiveness is refusing to allow the past to rob us anymore by letting our tears fall, our hearts to be heard and our breath filled with love to bathe our souls into re-birthing and allowing our beautiful strength and empowerment to unfold.

We never get more than we can handle. I know this can sound brutal, insensitive and downright mean.

Our struggles are a testament to the vastness of our strength and the bravery of our spirit that in one way or another potentially chose to overcome such challenges to heal, release, and transform.

Everything we need to heal lives within us and as we forgive the past, we create a present made on clear intentions to be happy and healed instead of simply costing on echoing reactionary pain from yesteryear.

When the timing is right and we're ready to truly release the past so we may truly heal, it is forgiveness that unchains us from the past so we can be free to start anew.

I believe in our true *strength*. I believe in our true *healing*!

We create today.
We create tomorrow.

!

CHAPTER 7
Dis Me? MISS ME!

Okay, it's now time to lighten up and shake off what no longer serves us in a playful somewhat silly fashion!

Once we've forgiven and accepted the situation as a lesson/teacher on our path and searched for the diamonds in the bullshit, then it's time to brush off the dust and pick ourselves up off the ground.

A fun remedy I've always enjoyed which sounds super childish and silly but can be a lot of fun and the best way to repair the feelings of abandonment or rejection is this:

If you dis me.... You're going to MISS me!

~ ~ ~ ~ ~ ~ ~ ~ ~ ~ Super silly right? ~ ~ ~ ~ ~ ~ ~ ~ ~ ~

I know but really, there is no need to take life's brilliant wisdom for knowing what is truly for our greatest good, hardships and all, personally.

Instead of feeling like we need to prove ourselves to anyone, we can take the hardships as an opportunity to *UPGRADE* our mind, body and soul.

Instead of letting the "dis" get us down we can choose to fall in love with ourselves, not in a cocky way but a liberating celebratory way of saying, ~YES~ to our own greatness.

They don't think I'm shiny? Sounds like a perfect time to perfect my *SHINE*!

I'm not talking about becoming a giant ego. I'm talking about LOVE. Loving ones' self and allowing ones' self to be celebrated in LOVE, support, and inspiration; freeing ourselves to be playful instead of allowing ourselves to be shamed by apparent obstacles.

It creates a playful space of rediscovering our own inner and outer beauty while taking our power back and saying, "*YES! I AM WORTH MORE*... than I have allowed myself to realize up to this point and I now choose to take the time to care truly for myself."

I NOW chose to celebrate and cultivate this beauty because there is no need to wait for "acknowledgment" from an outside source.

It's all about seeing and polishing our own diamond, and when we are still in a place of hurt and pain it makes it fun to say; well, when they're ready to see my beauty great but I've got no reason to wait.

I only have time to celebrate and cultivate the *AWESOMENESS* within.

Lets' face it, its' fun to turn up the *SEXY*, the *TALENT*, the *SHINE*, the *HEALTH, WEALTH,* and *PROSPERITY*...
                    And here's the thing; it *WORKS!*

If you dis me, you're going to MISS me, is all about not waiting for or needing anyone else to *SHINE!*

You can even use this when you see yourself dis~ing on yourself~ ha!

~ ~ ~ ~The possibilities are endless! ~ ~ ~ ~ ~
Again this isn't about proving yourself to anyone else. It's about saying yes to your beauty and committing to the love and beauty *within you* while in the challenge of feeling judged as lesser or insignificant and choosing to walk playfully in the direction of love!

It's about taking the intense energy of abandonment and judgment and choosing to transfer the intensity into productive self-love fuel; this works with all forms of feeling rejected or misjudged in any way.

Didn't get the job opportunity or whatever it was; *UPGRADE!*

Turn up the *SHINY* by activating your *MAGNETISM* and let them come to *YOU!*

And here's the thing, if you don't see how shiny you are, no one else will or even if they do, you will not believe them when they express how shiny you are to them.

We have to lick our wounds and love ourselves unconditionally and brush off the feelings of being unworthy and take the polar opposite reigns by honoring our beauty and strength in all our pluses and minuses within our perfect imperfections.

Once again, this is not to prove anyone wrong but to simply say yes to ourselves by taking the steps that we *DO* actually have control over to create happiness in our lives.

There is nothing more sexy and defiant than true happiness and fulfillment from saying yes we are worth it!

And again, no one is perfect! Perfectionism is not the goal; being healed and enjoying happiness is. It would be SO boring if we were all perfect all the time.

If life, love or the cosmos knocks you down, pick yourself up and say thank you for the inspiration to *GROW.*

Learning to grow beyond our weaknesses can be the most exciting and inspiring thing. Here's the thing; we will never stop learning and growing. If we think we have learned it all, then we need to go back to the beginning of the line because we've missed the most important thing of all!

There is always room to *GROW* and to humble ourselves to the vast ~*AWE*~ of possibilities and gems that are here to inspire, teach and help us to cultivate a greater understanding of our every changing world and our ever-changing selves.

Exercise:

Ask yourself, if I had my dream come true what would be different?

Within your senses, how would you notice this change?

What would you see, feel, hear, smell, taste that would be different?

You may just be surprised by how close your dreams are to coming true when you focus on the things you *CAN* actually change.

What can you do to create these kinds of experiences today?

CHAPTER 8
Date Yourself
~ Damnit! ~

Hey good looking, what ya got cooking?

So now that we've gotten a little playful with the dis me, MISS me, now it's time to really have some *FUN!*

The skinny is this, if we don't believe we deserve the truest bluest love we will never manifest it or if we do, we are likely to sabotage it.

How can we explore this further?

It's all about really getting to know ourselves.
I like to say, *"Date Yourself- Damnit!"* Get to know yourself in the ways that you open yourself to your lovers, friends, and loved ones. Get to know YOU.

What does this mean?

I encourage my clients to take a vow of dating themselves via being single *intentionally* for three to six months. When we take the time to truly fine-dine ourselves in the realms of love and explore ourselves in love; we open our vision and receptors to love in ways previously blocked by our tunnel vision focused outwardly away from ourselves and instead projecting on others.

Exploring our inner lover, our twin flame, the essence we long to share is essential if we want to grow in our ability to love and sincerely receive love instead of merely repeating our lessons in love.

There is no promised end-result in love because it's every changing, a constant cycle of learning as we expand and contract and expand again just like our heartbeat.

Honoring and cultivating unconditional love from within helps us to have courage and clarity in love that allows us to dive deep, within ourselves and our partners. The point is to be complete by the process of loving and not the projections and promises of love that are impossible to live up to especially if we live in a daydream of love and not the sometimes brutal truth and honesty of love.

This soul searching process can also be explored while already in a relationship and can be a great experience to share together by intentionally taking some time to do a little soul-searching by exploring within ourselves and our inner-most feelings and ideas about love and sharing this with our partner/s.

Either with a partner or solo, taking the time to look at ourselves and how we interact and respond in love is such a powerful eye opener.

In most relationships, we are constantly looking at our partner to mirror us in some way and looking for their signals of happiness or frustration to read where we are.

Taking the time to really look at how we explore, interact and play or do NOT explore, interact and play in love can be extremely enlightening as to how we create the pluses and the minuses we feel from our current situation.

We are so use to blaming our partners for where we are feeling unfulfilled in our relationships but most of the time if we looked closer we'd see we play a big hand in our own creation of the situation; again we are powerful creators, and this is actually really good news.

I always thought of myself as a hopeless romantic, always wearing my heart on my sleeve and wondering why I always felt like a victim in love.

During a vow of dating myself, I quickly could see that I was choosing the wrong partners who were obviously not right for me and the relationship I truly desired.

After taking a deep look at my patterns, I could clearly see that these situations were fulfilling my need to play the role of a romantic but all the while serving a greater purpose; keeping me safe from my bigger fear... my fear of intimacy and love.

Taking the time to authentically look at how we open up or close off to love is such a fascinating journey. Looking at how we are in love can truly open our ability to explore, manifest and experience love.

There are so many questions to explore and here's the thing, exploring these questions with complete and total honesty can genuinely open our world to love like we've never embraced it before.

Love is one of the most expansive tools of our galaxy; there is always room to grow in love; ALWAYS!

In love and life, in general, we tend not to see and embrace ourselves with the same eyes and heart we look into our lover's eyes with. When we look into a mirror we see the zits, the wrinkles, puffy eyes and the imperfect this, that and the other all the while never really giving our SOUL a glance.

We look in the mirror and judge and quickly make a few adjustments to trick the outside world into our doctored beauty, and we're out the door.

If we were to say the things we think to ourselves while looking in the mirror or any of our negative mental chatter to our loved ones, we'd quickly be labeled as abusive.

Our eyes are the gates to our soul. It is rare that we allow ourselves a moment to glance at what we so openly share with the rest of the world.

One of the first steps to getting to know ourselves in the realms of love is to begin to see ourselves as the twin flame that we are and open up to our own unique beauty.

I teach my clients to moonlight the mirror until their judgments fade, and their souls come out to play as they soul gaze with themselves in the mirror.

Many may read this and think this is egotistical self-worship but connecting with our soul via eye gazing in the mirror is anything but that.

This exercise can be extremely difficult for many but one of the most beautiful experiences once they've let themselves in.

When we truly allow ourselves to see ourselves in the realms of love and to honor ourselves for the first time without all the negative judgments, allowing ourselves to see the beauty we offer so freely to the one's we love, this opens our hearts to receive our beauty in an extremely healing way.

For some this is the very first time they've allowed themselves to see their own BEAUTY.

Although this is an extremely simple exercise, it gets the most resistance; this is where the tears naturally flow because this is what most of us don't want to face... ourselves.

We want to think our way into our strengths and hold walls of strength to mask the deeper more fragile feelings we feel a little too vulnerable for feeling. But that's just it, we have to put the judgment down and face ourselves with the same unconditional love we give our nearest and dearest and bath in that love that we ARE to begin truly healing.

We CAN choose to open our eyes to viewing our world from a space of unconditional love; consciously operating from our hearts center.

There are so many lonely people out there who feel like they have nobody, and when they look in the mirror, they see a "nobody".

If they would just give themselves a chance and look deeper into their own eyes with the same open heart they long to share with someone, "special" they'd soon recognize that someone extremely special is looking back at them every time they look in the mirror.

By recognizing and acknowledging that someone special in the mirror, it then activates their ability to see the sea of connection gracefully waiting to be embraced in each and every moment.

We must start by loving ourselves unconditionally and allowing for the deepest parts of ourselves to be held and healed by the magic of unconditional Love's transformational light.

With practice the once lonely souls would soon see that they have the perfect partner for creating all things awesome always right there in front of them staring back at them in the mirror.

The empowering fact is they truly do have the ability to co-create incredibly fulfilling relationships if only they'd see that their relationship with themselves was the most important key!

So yeah, "Date Yourself -Damnit!"

I like to encourage my clients to actually take themselves out on dates even. Not in their jeans and a baggy shirt but to spice it up! Get your sexy on and take yourself somewhere special, perhaps a museum or for a romantic walk on the beach or to a nice restaurant and genuinely enjoy being with yourself. It's okay to notice whatever attention you might get with your sexy on but truly do this for you and not outside attention.

Feel into the space that is YOU. Feel the inspiration from within and notice what brings you happiness and joy about being in your own unique PRESENCE.

Notice what you enjoy about yourself. There is nothing sexier than being comfortable in your own skin; this is an excellent exercise for getting to experience ourselves in our MAGNETISM.

We can create a lot of happiness for ourselves if we simply *CHOOSE* to. When we care for, honor and cherish ourselves, we then can realize we have everything that we truly need to create incredible love and happiness from within.

When we experience the beauty of unconditional self-love, we then can begin to open up to giving and receiving love in the most expansive non-needy ways which is incredibly exciting and attractive because it becomes more about the journey with our special ones and not the needing someone else to fill our gaps.

We must learn to fill our own cups with the most gorgeous magnetic sparkling love and drink this transformational love in.

If a three to six-month vow of dating yourself or exploring yourself in love is too ominous, how about just starting with one week?

Start the day by stating,
"I choose to love myself today because_____."
And go get your sexy on for YOU, not for outside attention but to simply feel incredible in your own skin.

Life is meant to be a blast, and it's filled with treasure pretty much on the constant if you have the awareness for it!

The problem is we've been trained not to see that we *ARE Heaven on Earth* and as soon as we *DECIDE* to make the shift into this awareness, things get pretty *MAGICAL!*

Exercise:

Look deeply into the mirror and allow your eyes to soften their gaze. Breathe deeply into your heart and allow yourself to be seen through the eyes of unconditional love and embrace the whole of you. Be gentle with yourself and the truth of you that may come out.

Allow yourself to unconditionally love yourself just as you are in this present moment.

Now ask yourself,

- Who am I in love?

- What does love mean to me?

- In Love I am....?

- I hide from love when...?

- I open to love how and when....?

- I have blocked love in what ways?

- I am an amazing lover how, when and why?

- I am unable to love how, when and why?

- I grow in love where?

- I hide from love how, when and where?

- What does it mean to love?

- Who am I as a lover?

- What does being a lover mean to me?

Answer these questions in the mirror and/or write your answers down.

This is a great exercise to revisit as we shift and transform into new lessons, growths and experiences.

Exploring ourselves in love is a beautifully empowering *lifetime* pursuit, thankfully so!

CHAPTER 9
MAGNETIC POWER

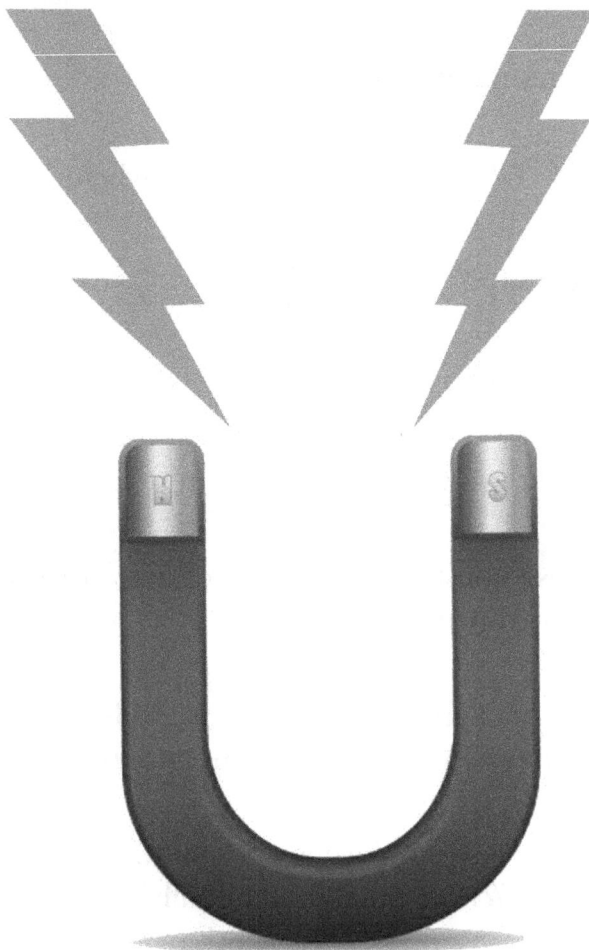

Most of us focus on the, "I don't/s".

I don't want this... I don't like this, that or the other...
I don't have this, that or the other... I don't believe it's
possible ... I don't trust... I don't think I can.....

And this is where we are putting all of our POWER!

When we get caught up in the worry and the panic,
we are essentially energetically rooting for what we
don't want.

When we are in a state or an emotional imprint, we
send out a powerful energetic magnetic signal that
then attracts whatever it is the state is and thus fueling
it into being.

When we focus on the, "not" and the, "don't" we are
inviting "it" to get comfortable. We will never see
what we haven't yet energetically invested in and
believed into possibility. If we believe we don't
deserve whatever it is; we will block and sabotage
whatever it is to validate these inner feelings.

WHAT WE BELIEVE WE ACHIEVE!

If all we do is see, feel and think in the minus zone then we will simply only attract minus zone experiences, essentially getting good at playing in the minus zone so much that it becomes our comfort zone.

All worthy extraordinary journeys are anything but comfortable. If comfort is what we are seeking then, we need to keep all our complaints to ourselves about how stuck in the mud we may feel. We are the ones responsible for putting ourselves there; as hard as this may sound; we are responsible for taking the steps to get ourselves out of it; plain and simple.

We are the ones who must make the shift. The first step is to decide we are done with playing the losing game of victim role-playing and then it's time to commit to putting action into our step! We have everything we need deep within us; we must trust this and decide to commit to our greatness.

All the possibilities of the universe live within us.
Believe into this.
Feel it's SPARK!

Follow your heart as it opens and unfolds the path to YOU in your clarity, empowerment, your happiness, and joy.

It is mandatory to stretch your comfort zone if you are to truly GROW!

-Fact!

I'm sure learning to walk wasn't necessarily easy or comfortable, but the excitement to get up and moving around motivated us into *ACTION*. It's in focusing on what we truly want that magnetizes our abilities to grow, adapt and create comfort in new and exciting zones.

If you walk around just avoiding the, "I don't(s)" you will be incredibly overwhelmed by them and be so energetically zapped that you will have nothing to give the, "I DO's!" Your focus on the, "don't" will also be actively attracting the "don't ('s)" too.

- *What's shiny to you?*

- *What gives you a spark?*

- *What energizes you when you think about it?*

- *What calls you to take ACTION?*

The energy is there for a reason; it's a part of you calling and inviting you to step it up into a new sense of adventure and grace.

It's in the, "I DO's" that the MAGIC lives!

I do have these tools within my grasp. I do have resources I can utilize to learn that which I haven't yet learned to create the means to get from A to B and so forth.

I do have the ability to breathe in this breath of life and have gratitude for being alive in this present moment.

I do have whatever it is that you DO have and by actually honoring what you DO have you can create anything from there, but you need all your energy in the DO's if you want to...

DO GREAT THINGS!

Also, you can't have what you do not bless someone else to have or receive. We are all ONE in the big picture. What you curse another for having or what may appear, in your judgment, to be more than enough only puts a limit on your own ability to receive.

If you want to be the judge of what measurements are acceptable regarding attainment, all you are doing is simply creating energetic blocks to the unlimited flow of the universe by creating a wall of stagnating judgment where the boundlessness of the universe cannot flow because you are in resistance to it.

If you want it, you've got to bless it to anyone and everyone; plain and simple. We are all one. What you love and hate about another is simply what you love or hate about yourself.

Do you want more abundance? Celebrate those who are abundant in your world. Are you feeling in the minus zone in the romance department? Instead of being one of the many who say those lovebirds make me sick; be the one that blesses and celebrates them thus inviting that sweet lovebird energy into your world instead of repelling it because you can't seem to bless someone else to having and embracing it.

YOU

are a
~~~~~~~~~~~*MAGNET!* ~~~~~~~~~~~

You pull into your field plus (+) and minus (-) experiences to learn and grow from. Not all challenging situations are bad, evil or non-evolved.

Just because things don't feel amazing, fun or exciting, doesn't mean they aren't here to teach us the most valuable treasures hidden within the experience.

Stepping up to the plate and owning whatever it is for good, not evil is the essence of empowerment!

The biggest transformational tool in one's toolbox is *PERCEPTION;* which is completely capable of turning everything and anything either into GOLD or shit... *you decide!*

How you view an event or situation has everything to do with how it holds and/or EMPOWERS you into clearer more intention based choices.

We CAN choose to see through eyes that see challenges in exciting new ways, and this includes the past, present, and future challenges.

If we choose to do the work to heal internal obstacles within the subconscious, the very act of facing them with the intent to heal robs them of their previous grasp; this in turn transforms the entire experience because we cannot return to a previous viewpoint once we've expanded our horizons.

Our field of perception automatically expands with the new awareness and one cannot return to the same dimension of understanding because it simply would no longer fit and serve us in the same ways.

We must trust our magnetism. Wherever we are... we are precisely where we need to be for whatever lesson/growth we need to experience. Yes!

Trust!

Trust in your magnetism and own it.

+ Positive and Negative –

Why did I magnetize this challenge?
What underlying belief does it serve?

All the negatives are here in one way or another to fulfill a positive purpose. Life would be so boring if there were nothing to overcome.

It is in the contrast and conflict that gives us the opportunity to see what we are made of; which is always far greater than we naturally envision for ourselves.

~~~~~~~TRUST! ~~~~~~~~~~

Again this is where we can learn to find the

DIAMONDS in the Bullshit.

What is there for me to learn from this difficulty?

The sooner we see the power of our choices the better. We can choose to empower ourselves and others by the choices we make. We can begin to see that we always have powerful choices within our grasp available to us if we choose to see with clarity that which we are meant to learn and grow from that pushes us beyond the comfort zone.

We can consciously choose a new course of action for ourselves in the here and now.... ALWAYS!
Especially after consciously owning our magnetism!

Once we have nothing more to learn from the challenge, we can move on to new and exciting challenges. If older challenges return, for whatever reason, it is simply a reminder to shift into deeper clarity and understanding owning our power of being the creator of the situation, all the while holding a space of non-judgment; opening to unconditional love and expansive growth.

Saying, "I do!" to the difficulty, is saying, "I do!" to SUCCESS.

Saying yes, I do own responsibility for this. I refuse to play the victim but instead choose to empower myself to be accountable for whatever this is and by doing so we can truly own our power to create that which we seek in the here and now.

Exercise:

Write an honest list of where you place blame and responsibility on someone else for your grief and/or discomfort.

Ask yourself,
"How is this serving me? How can putting all the blame on someone else create empowering change for my life?"

Putting the ball in someone else's court simply means you now have given them the control and put yourself and your transformation on the waiting list while you wait for them to clear the slate or whatever it is you desire of them.

Unfortunately, one can go an entire lifetime without ever getting the other/s to show up to do the work.

Okay, now that you have a list of the wrongdoers simply write a letter to them and say your truth and powerfully own your end of the responsibility. Send it or not... it's up to you.

There is always something you could have done differently; that would have created a different effect on you and the outcome.

Learn from this and choose to see it clearly so you don't have to keep bumping into the same issues and problems.

Clear intent and responsibility will always WIN.

That fire burned me...... Damn that fire! I touched it, and it was hot. Curse that flame.

Next time we will be sure to handle the fire with care. We are the creator of the lessons that flow our way! OWN IT!

Now write a list of the, "I do's"!

Take inventory of what you already have going for yourself and fill your heart with deep gratitude for what you already have.

Now write a list that really honors what you have to be grateful for and what you bring to the table.

Honor the gifts you have in this present moment; this activates an awareness of the treasure available to us in any given moment; once we have the eyes to see these new treasures, all the sudden new treasures make themselves known.

Trust into this. Believe into this.

CHAPTER 10
What We BELIEVE
~We ACHIEVE! ~

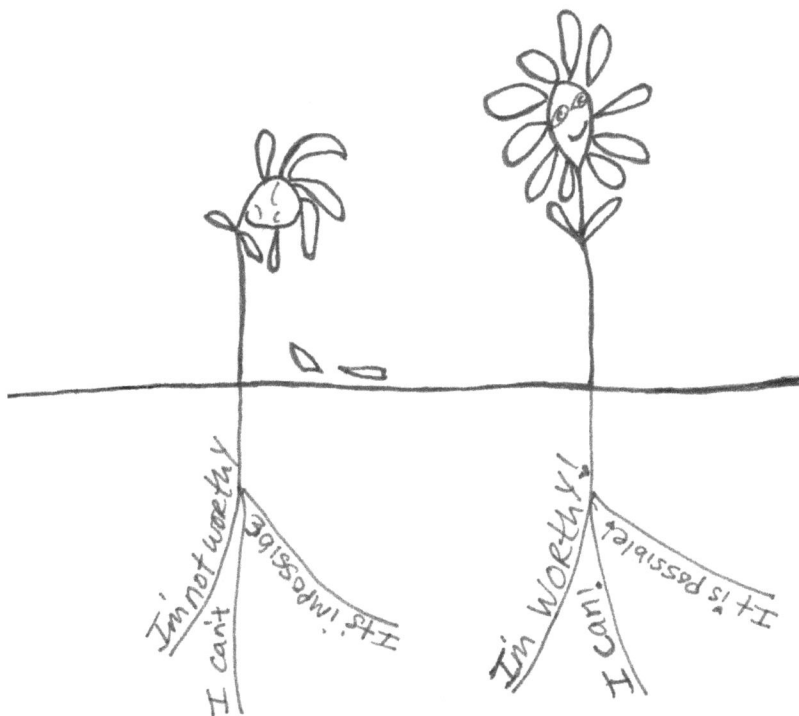

"What you're thinking is what you're *becoming*."
- Muhammad Ali

My biggest belief is in the POWER OF BELIEF! *What we believe we ACHIEVE.* What we think, feel and experience paints our perspective of reality whether we are conscious of it or not. We think we create our reality consciously when it's actually created mostly subconsciously.

Our belief system is stored in our subconscious mind. What we believe subconsciously (which may very well contradict what we think we believe) is what we create.

Our subconscious mind is our grand library where all of our data including our beliefs, emotions, experiences and expectations are stored.

Our subconscious is our internal hard drive that simply runs the data of our current operating system. It is essentially our automatic pilot.

If we are wondering what is going on within our subconscious mind, all we have to do is take a look at our lives and observe our patterns. Quickly we can see where we may have blocks and limiting beliefs subconsciously blocking us from receiving greater happiness and well-being in our lives.

If we are seeing mostly the negative and are mainly listening to negative self-talk, we are creating a large file of negativity for our automatic subconscious pilot.

The subconscious then steers us in the direction of negative experiences to validate these internal expectations and beliefs. Luckily, same goes for thinking positively!

An amazing example of the sheer magnitude of possibility within this concept is demonstrated beautifully in the medical documentation and exploration of a man endearingly named, "The Incredible Mr. Wright", found in the Psychological variables in human cancer, Journal of Protective Techniques, 21, 331-340 by Bruno Klopfer.

Mr. Wright was on his deathbed with tumors the size of oranges. To what must have seemed to be a miracle to Mr. Wright an experimental drug that soon proved to be worthless but in *his* eyes seemed to be his last hope, was being researched in the very hospital he was likely to have his last breaths. Because of his pleas he was entered reluctantly into the study where he proved to be the *only* one with promising results.

His tumors vanished and within less than two weeks he checked out of the hospital with no signs of his previous disease.

Months later learning from the media of the failures of the "miracle drug" he quickly returned to the previous conditions of the life-threatening disease.

With nothing left to offer him his doctor experimented by telling Mr. Wright not to believe the media and that a new version of the drug that was much more powerful was coming in, and this was sure to help him return to perfect health like he had already experienced. After administering what essentially is a placebo, Mr. Wright quickly returned to a perfect state of health.

Once again month's later news hit the media calling the drug an utter failure, and this sent Mr. Wright to his final return to the disease that killed him within days of the news.

Mr. Wright's incredible story demonstrates how powerful our focus and beliefs can be in affecting and creating what unfolds in our realities.

The mind-body connection cannot and should not be ignored!

The sheer power of the placebo effect demonstrates the pure essence of healing that lives within us. To label it as a fluke because Big Pharma can't make money on it is a disgrace to our humanity. The power of the placebo has been the one constant and should be honored and researched with more dedication and complete and utter respect for the power, and gifts that it holds.

Big Pharma can't profit from this kind of healing but humanity can!

It's time for us to take our *POWER* back! We can empower ourselves by dedicating an awareness to our daily practices within our minds, bodies, and spirits creating greater health and well-being in respects to the power we *do* have within our choices.

We can create a new healing path for our humanity as we discover new ways of empowering our thoughts and how we treat and respect our physical, mental, emotional, and spiritual bodies.

ALL of our bodies; our minds, our physical bodies, and souls are connected; they are one, the whole of our being. Acting as if these parts of ourselves are separate creates the dysfunction we experience as a disease, conflict, and despair. We must learn to honor and embrace ourselves and each other as a whole; a network which is learning to work together to create harmony.

Western medicine likes to separate mind and body which is impossible in reality because they are one. You won't find one without the other.

We breathe, our blood pumps, we digest food all without any conscious effort thankfully so; our subconscious makes it all happen on the automatic.

Imagine trying to go to sleep all the while worried about forgetting to breathe as we slept: again, mind and body are one; our subconscious mind cares for these needs automatically, so we don't have to.

If our subconscious mind can run all of our automatic bodily functions, you better believe it has the complete power to heal and transform our bodies, our minds, our emotions and our behaviors.

Especially when dealing with an illness, the subconscious had something to do with its creation, so it is the most powerful place to do the work in healing the internal conflict.

I had to face the awareness of this powerful truth as I awoke from a colonoscopy with a Doctor screaming in my face informing me that I, in fact, had a giant tumor and that they would need to do emergency surgery right away.

Filled with deep gratitude for my training as a medical hypnotherapist, I never once filled with the normal fear based media induced response of, "Oh my God, I'm going to die!"

I instead simply felt anger and sadness for my fellow man, woman, and child who had also awoken to such intense bedside manners. I felt compassion and a sense of protection for those who hadn't the knowledge I had to focus completely on healing and avoid listening to such fear-based energy. I thought to myself; there's no way I'm going to heal this challenge if I listen to the fear he's pumping out at me right now!

I quickly informed him that I was a hypnotherapist and that my subconscious mind was listening to every single word they were saying when I was "under" and they had better be *POSITIVE* regardless of what they find in me!

As they rolled my hospital bed back into my room, they told my mother to make sure to let me know that they were positive!

Especially when it comes to overcoming some of the most intense challenges of life, it is utterly vital that we put all of our energy on what it is that we WANT to create. Not that we should ignore or judge our feelings of being overwhelmed, weak, and scared, but to honor our being in all of its needs by reaching out for help to face what we don't want to see so we can bring it to light where it can heal and transform.

Dealing with an issue at its roots subconsciously empowers us to heal and create awareness in our depths, so our automatic pilot is on the same healing path that we have consciously chosen for ourselves.

What we believe we achieve.

If the results we are searching for are eluding us within our conscious efforts, there's likely a subconscious block. Thankfully this can be resolved with ease when addressed via deep relaxation, also known as Trance.

I knew it was a crystal clear, no other option but to heal, pure intention approach that was the only way through my challenge of cancer, so I rooted this CELLULAR*DIVINITY empowerment into my subconscious via self-hypnosis.

I had to learn to LOVE myself deeply and completely within my subconscious. I had to learn to stop sacrificing myself and to really love every part of my being like I was an innocent new born child so I could allow the healing into every cell in my body, mind and soul and say yes to the healing and most importantly, say yes to my worthiness of healing.

This meant truly facing the places within me that felt unworthy of healing; it was in facing and embracing those parts of me that I was able to truly become whole again.

We've been taught to take it all on and sacrifice ourselves but to truly honor one another we must honor ourselves all the way down to our cells. This is what I call Cellular Divinity, loving each and every cell as sacred.

When we honor ourselves down to our very cells this is where we really begin to activate the healing potential and possibility of our humanity.

Especially when we are coming from abuse, we tend to believe that we somehow deserved it because in many cases we tend to trust or have trusted those who have violated us; so we blame ourselves sometimes down to our very cells and this is where we need to send powerful unconditional love and embrace the innocence we've caged within for not being strong enough, good enough, smart enough, deserving enough, the list is endless... we have to love ourselves all the way down to every cell to set these parts of ourselves free and to reclaim our worthiness to heal, whatever it is!

The way out is through; you have to BELIEVE you can do it to get there! It is so important that we believe we are worthy of our goals and heal any blocks that may hold us back from receiving them.

BELIEVE and get the support you need!

You deserve it!

No matter what kind of challenge you are going through you are going to need support to overcome some obstacles. Getting the support we need and asking for help and guidance is strength, not weakness.

We are all here to help one another.

Each of us is placed near the other to learn, grow, and heal.

It is a GIFT to be able to help someone in need and show up for our fellow humanity.

Giving is receiving. Receiving is giving. Like the ebb and flow of our breath and the tides of the sea, it is our natural rhythm and flow.

Seeking this balance is the key to health, wealth, happiness, and success.

~ ~ ~ ~ ~ What we BELIEVE we achieve. ~ ~ ~ ~ ~

- *Believe in your Health!*

- *Believe in your Wealth!*

- *Believe in your Happiness!*

- *Believe in YOU!*

- *Believe you are WORTH it!*

- *Believe you are Worthy!*

- *Believe you can HEAL whatever it is!*

- *Believe you CAN!*

- *Believe in your Heart and your Dreams!*

- *Believe in your Gifts and share them with the rest of us unashamedly!*

CHAPTER 11
{HIP~IN THE KNOW~SIS}
~ *HYPNOSIS* ~

For some reason which I believe is more about controlling us than anything else, we've been handed the fearful imprint of an evil hypnotist making us do something that is humiliating, embarrassing or revealing. I see this image repeatedly in children's cartoons still to this day just as I did when I was a child.

Oddly , as a society, we've been "hypnotized" into a societal trance to view the very act of humiliation, embarrassment and total mockery of a fellow human being as a source of entertainment via the ever popular "reality shows". As if these PROGRAMS have anything real to offer us about reality. These programs are a perfect example of the very toxic roll-fulfillment programming which acts sadly as role models for our children who've been raised by the television screen. This media behavior creates more beliefs about separation, war and who's the mightiest of them all is who we want to be if we are to survive.

We must look beyond this fear based societal programming if we are to grow and create a beautiful, liberated humanity.

This seed of fear programmed into our society about hypnosis couldn't be further from the truth of how hypnosis and hypnotherapy work.

Hypnosis is a natural state that we go in and out of without being aware of it several times a day when we daydream or are in the zone. When we are in a "trance", we are actually in a heightened state of awareness and focused control. It is very much a state of heightened and concentrated learning.

In this non-stop inundated information age, we are more hypnotized than ever! We operate mostly on automatic pilot, so the real question is this; are we in a trance that is working for us?

Or *against* us?

Hypnosis and Hypnotherapy access the subconscious mind through trance also known as deep relaxation. As we relax and quiet our conscious minds, we enable ourselves to access our subconscious mind where our current life's blueprint is stored.

If we want to create dynamic change, it is by accessing and transforming the data within the subconscious that will create the most effective results.

The subconscious has no opinion or judgment it simply holds, protects and runs the data regardless if the data is good, bad, serving or defeating.

When we try to make changes via charging forward with our will-power, this is the long and potentially impossible way around. Our will power lives within our conscious minds which isn't the mind in charge of our habits or our higher power.

We can make changes as long as we keep extremely focused on the changes we are creating but as soon as we slip into distractions the subconscious will shift back into automatic pilot returning to past habits and programs that may no longer serve us.

Our conscious minds are amazing and brilliant, and we very much need our logical conscious mind to know what we are experiencing and what we truly desire so we can plan manifesting these desires.

Unfortunately, our conscious mind is apt to paint an expectation from past experiences. It doesn't realize it is operating from a limited perspective that may be influenced from someone else's limited imprint on us from our informative years or some past experiences.

I like to say," If you like your conscious mind, just wait until you experience your subconscious and SUPERCONSCIOUS Mind!"

Our subconscious mind is our goal oriented mind here to serve the program according to the data within its library; it has no judgment or opinion so it will run both the data that serves us AND destroys us.

To truly create dynamic and permanent change working with the subconscious mind can create the most powerful results and with ease.

Hypnosis uses the hypnotic state to quiet what is known as the critical faculty through Trance; this is where a good hypnotist shines!

Up until around four years of age, we are very much in a hypnotic state easily soaking up all the information and data around us; this can be extremely helpful but can also be not so good depending on our environments at this pivotal time.

This highly hypnotic stage is why children don't have to be taught to speak their native languages they just soak up the knowledge and they can easily learn other languages and soak up all sorts of information at this time; basically it all sinks in like a sponge.

As we have our first experiences input into our subconscious libraries a barrier between our conscious and subconscious mind begins to formulate, and this is what is known as the critical faculty.

Our critical faculty acts as a guard for our subconscious mind. The critical faculty seeks approval from the subconscious for new information to get through. If our subconscious mind has a large file that supports the idea, the subconscious mind allows the information through.

On the other hand, if there isn't a large file on the desired shift but instead conflicting data then the critical faculty will reject the information while the subconscious creates excuses why the information can't get through to support the larger data files.

Through TRANCE, we can lull the critical faculty offline while engaging the subconscious mind to access the data and transform limiting beliefs into productive ones that serve our highest good. Again, trance is a heighten state of learning and concentration so we get to choose what is for our highest good.

Once the transformational work is complete, and the critical faculty comes back online, it will then now protect the new empowering data! ~TADA!

It's like upgrading your operating system, once you've installed the new program; it's the only program it runs. If it's stored in the subconscious the critical faculty will protect it, again good or bad, this is why doing the work is so important.

Would you rather choose which subconscious files run your life or simply hope all the best data got in and roll with the punches?

You wouldn't want just any operating system on your computer right? Same goes for your subconscious library.

The mistake a lot of people tend to make when utilizing hypnosis or doing any transformation work for that matter is they expect instant results.

If there isn't an instant fix, they discontinue the work needed to cultivate the results they seek.

Here's the thing, our negative patterns, habits, beliefs, and expectations have taken a lifetime to create their data files. Self-discovery and transformational healing unfold exactly when we are ready, like a rose, each petal closer to the core beautifully guiding our way.

It takes time to do the work and sometimes not very much time at all. Very much like a seed planted in the darkness of the soil, if the seed hadn't the patience and perseverance but instead wanted instant gratification it would never reach its' bloom.

Everything takes practice and the more we focus on and commit to healing the sooner we will see and feel the results. The responsibility is on us to do our personal work. That said, many of my clients have shifted right into the gear of their chosen desire; things come when they are meant, and your *super*-conscious mind knows better than anyone what's best for YOU.

Once we've grasped the strength, power, and role of our subconscious minds; choosing to work with our subconscious becomes an easy choice.

Our subconscious and SUPERCONSCIOUS is essentially our core that knows the best and fastest route to healing, transforming and rewriting our data programs.

Hypnosis simply reroutes our automatic pilot, so it's in alignment with our clear and personal choices while releasing the conditioning from our past and the baggage we've been handed to carry.

Exercise: Self-Hypnosis

- This exercise is meant for a time when you can fully relax, without distractions.
- Never practice self- hypnosis when driving or operating heavy machinery.
- Make sure your cell phone ringer is off and that anyone who might knock on your door knows not to at this time.
- First step is to get clear on your goal for self-hypnosis.
- Pick <u>one</u> goal to use at a time and be very clear with your words as to the results you are seeking.
- See, feel, hear and taste the end result.
- What would it be like to achieve your goal?
- What would be new or different?
- Once you are clear on your goal write it down as a simplified affirmation.

Examples:

I sleep deeply and with ease.

I am confidant, focused and clear.

I am a happy and confidant non-smoker.

I reach for nutrient rich foods to support my fit and healthy body.

-

- Once you are clear on your goal and have stepped into the end result and chosen your words of intention, then it's simply time to relax.

- Find the most comfortable position for your body making sure your spine is nice and straight and fully supported.

- Simply notice your breath and as you notice your breath, the act of being aware of your breath automatically deepens your breath as the inhale slows down smoothly and the exhale relaxes you more deeply each breath.

- As you allow your breath to relax you more and more, you may choose to start to count backwards from 99 and going deeper and deeper into relaxation with each number. If you'd like, you may see, feel or sense in whatever way, a beautiful staircase that is completely safe and secure, and as you count down you can go deeper down the stairs and as you go deeper and deeper down, relaxing more and more with each breath, you'll notice you find yourself in a very peaceful and relaxing trance.

- As you notice this deep relaxation/trance you may begin to set your intentions/goal.

Simply state: **<u>Subconscious mind show me</u>**:

    - How to sleep deeply and with ease.

    - How to be confident focused and clear.

    - I AM a happy and confident non-smoker.

    - How to reach for healthy nutrient rich foods to support my fit and healthy body.

- And repeat saying the goal or whatever declarations of the goal and repeat it as you go, deeper and deeper, being open to guidance that may come in that helps you reach your goal.

- And when you are ready to come back you can simply start counting from 1 to 5 stating that you will be fully awake and ready for an amazing day or night depending on the circumstance and come back on the count of five wide awake, feeling great.

- You can always set a timer for twenty minutes or so when you first get started to help with your practice.

- Practice and repeat.

It is best to work with a hypnotherapist who can help you to reach the trance state and install helpful suggestions for you to be able to return to the trance state with ease.

Once you've explored the trance state with a professional it's easier to know where you are going and what to expect.

Start with a goal that is really important to you and stick with that goal for at least three weeks.

The more you practice self- hypnosis, the more connected you will be to your subconscious automatic pilot and can steer your life in the crystal clear direction of your choosing.

CHAPTER 12
SUPER-CONSCIOUS

Our **SUPERCONSCIOUS** lives within our subconscious; it is wisdom, love, compassion, expansion, and transformational healing.

Our **SUPERCONSCIOUS** mind protects us from harm so we will never have an experience via hypnosis, hypnotherapy, self-hypnosis or meditation that we aren't truly able to handle.

The subconscious knows what we need to experience to create the results we desire. That said it is imperative that we trust, feel safe and have a strong rapport with whomever we are working with to get the best results within this work.

If a challenging moment were to present itself while in a hypnotic state, there would be a choice in whether to experience it or simply witness the experience from a safe place so you can get the wisdom the experience is translating without having to experience the intensity of the experience. There is always a choice and the more we embrace this, the more we can choose EMPOWERMENT.

Our **SUPERCONSCIOUS** knows the perfect dose of an experience and never gives us anything we can't truly handle because it is our grand protector and knows what's best for our highest good. After all, it knows us best!

If we think of the societal programmed fear of the "deep dark secrets in the closet of our subconscious mind," it's our self-judgment (and /or past judgments from someone else and/or the suggestion that these deep dark secrets even exist from the media) that creates the fear, pain, and worry of these parts of ourselves.

If there is no opinion or judgment (which thankfully the subconscious mind has neither of these qualities!) to paint these feelings, thoughts and experiences as bad, it simply just becomes information that then can be used to ~en*LIGHT*en~ and illuminate areas where we feel darkness.

It is your empowerment waiting within your subconscious mind not the boogeyman! In fact, I believe the "boogeyman" is likely to have created the "idea" of the need to fear our subconscious minds, in order to keep us from the EMPOWERMENT gained from working with our subconscious mind. Knowledge is power, the more we explore our inner worlds the more we can empower and change our outer worlds.

Again, our SUPERCONSCIOUS minds are made up of, WISDOM, COMPASSION, UNCONDITIONAL LOVE, EXPANSION, AND TRANSFORMATIONAL HEALING which darkness simply can't win against because LOVE is always greater than darkness. Love knows that the darkness is simply the other side of light and LOVE can see through its scary masks to see the light on the other side, always illuminating the way!

This illumination creates space for a new awareness from the lessons from within to replace the confusion and misinformation that lead us to carry the judgment, fear, worry, pain or shame in the first place.

Most pain and suffering comes from holding wounds or pockets of judgment where we simply forgot to shine the light of love and instead chose to carry a cross or a scarlet letter instead of truly loving ourselves unconditionally so we can heal and learn from whatever it is.

Love will always win; it is the strongest frequency that will transform lower frequencies when activated at peak levels.

Most of us find it easier to fill our hearts with compassion for the ones we love and forgive them so they can release their wounds and heal. But as a society, we are taught to hold our embarrassing "weakness" deep within and to shame ourselves into ignoring these challenging wounds and instead put up a wall of strength, after all, we are meant to be perfect just like the models in the magazines right?

~~ It is in the value of vulnerability that our truest strengths SHINE. ~~

Acknowledging our inner wounds and honoring them by listening to them and hearing their needs, in turn, heals them creating a truly strong foundation; this, in turn, enables us to expand in our ability to GROW.

The more we heal and grow at our roots, the more compassion we have to share with our fellow humanity, animals, and the planet.

Getting to know this incredible source of transformation within us is the beginning of understanding that we are in fact the creators of our world and we can choose to live an extraordinary life.

There is always a choice, and we can always choose to heal, transform and be the masters of our reality.

One of the big reasons I'm writing this book is because I want to shine a ~LIGHT~ on what an incredibly empowering tool Hypnosis is. To just think of it as a tool to quit smoking or release weight is merely the tip of the iceberg regarding its applications. Although these results are beyond WONDERFUL, it is just the beginning of its abilities within transformation and creation of our desired outcomes.

Getting to know ourselves within the realms of hypnosis is such an incredible eye opener to our endless potential. Hypnosis is an incredible tool for getting to our core and embracing our potential and the totality of our being.

Hypnosis is not just a tool for problem-solving but can also be used quite powerfully for becoming more masterful and skilled in whatever it is we have our focused determination on manifesting.

I am constantly asked what I can accomplish with hypnosis and my response to this question is, "that's like asking, what can your brain do and accomplish?"

Hypnosis is a natural state where we get to access our subconscious minds to create the results we want from our subconscious automatic pilots.

Our subconscious mind is aware of our decisions 7 seconds before our conscious minds are. High-performance athletes, actors, artist and incredible minds in general simply learn to trust and engage with their subconscious minds to create outstanding results.

Our potential is truly endless! The more empowered we are, standing up to our greater selves by fulfilling our most desired potentials, the more we have to offer and empower our world, planet, and our humanity.

Beyond being a hypnotherapist, I am also a demolition coach.

Demolition what?

Yes, you heard me right, I'm a demolition coach! What this means is I use the incredibly powerful tools of Hypnosis, NLP, Life Coaching and Executive Coaching to help my clients demolish what is no longer serving them so they can make room to erect their truest hearts desires.

Yes, I said and meant ERECT! It is so important to be truly turned on to and by life, and we are the ones responsible for making this Happen!

When we demolish our internal and external blocks, we get to choose our new blueprints, structures, visions, dreams and purpose. When we get the support we need to demolish the past; we can activate the present and create an awe-inspiring today and tomorrow.

And now with pleasure, I'd like to introduce the incredible high-performance tool known as, Neuro-Linguistic-Programming.

NLP is the art of living a ~ *SUPERCONCIOUS* ~ life!

Although trance state is not needed to engage in NLP techniques and methodologies, it was partially birthed from studying and modeling Ericksonian hypnosis and is an accelerated way to create profound change within our conscious and subconscious mind.

We can create incredible change by actively engaging our conscious mind by using innovative techniques that expands awareness within our senses.

We can quite literally install new strategies and strengths using this incredible mental technology. It is debatable but I still believe NLP utilizes a trance state just the active awake aspect of the ability of trance. NLP stands for Neuro~Linguistic~Programming which is known as the study of EXCELLENCE!

- Neuro: our perceptual experiences through our senses and nervous system.
- Linguistics: our mental processes translated through language.
- Programming: our programs and patterns.

We can actively create a profound awareness of what excellence is by studying and modeling success.

By experiencing the attributes of success through our senses, our neurology, language and patterns we can become the essence of SUCCESS and mirror the results of those we look up to for inspiration and guidance.

We can assimilate success through modeling and by doing so we can learn to develop new habits, perceptions and ways of being and communicating from those who have mastered what we are seeking.

NLP gives us the tools and mental technologies needed to create outstanding results and with ease by learning HOW to use our mind, and senses to motivate ourselves. NLP helps us to master the art of communication which in turn produces incredible results.

I like to call NLP the *SAMURAI OF HYPNOSIS*. NLP takes the reigns of our perception by teaching and installing skills, strengths and awareness in order to create the very best results; much like the dedication of a samurai who uses precise skills and weaponry all with the purpose and intent to better themselves and walk in honor always seeking to further their mastery on all levels.

By actively improving ourselves with NLP we can quite literally become ultimate mind warriors, banishing stagnate thinking, feeling and behaving so we can master our minds and in turn perfect our realities, consciously and subconsciously cultivating our SUPERCONSCIOUS!

"If you can change the way you think, you can change the way you feel which changes what you can do!"
～Richard Bandler co-founder of NLP.

CHAPTER 13
The POWER OF
~IMAGINATION!~

"Every living being is an engine geared to the wheelwork of the universe. Though seemingly affected only by its immediate surroundings, the sphere of external influence extends to infinite distance."

Nikola Tesla

"You can't depend on your eyes... when your *IMAGINATION* is out of focus."

~Mark Twain

I like to get my clients daydreaming. They tend to respond to this at first as if it's a joke; I then ask them what day-dreams they've already experienced that day, and this becomes a great eye opener to how much we daydream but typically in a negative way.

Our imagination is the most powerful tool we have because it is *the language of our subconscious mind.* In many ways, we live in an imaginary world, a world created by our imaginations.

We imagine each morning how our day or week might unfold; imagining how much conflict or stress might happen if we don't do this, that or the other. We imagine what a person is like without actually meeting them. We imagine how others may perceive us and how they may react to certain situations. We imagine what someone may have thought in response to something we said or didn't say. We imagine all sorts of things all throughout the day.

In so many ways we have convinced ourselves out of happiness by our lack of positive imagination. We have made life so concrete that possibilities have no room to breathe or even be seen.

We imagine we are stuck, and that's just the way it is, after all, that's what we've learned along the way. If the past brought us pain why should we expect anything else, that's just not realistic.

"It ain't what you don't know that gets you into trouble. *It's what you know for sure that just ain't so."*
   -again another awesome quote from ~Mark Twain

In NLP, we model success because the goal is to strive for excellence... how do we do it? We study those who are successful and see what they are doing RIGHT! We focus on what it's like to have the attributes of success. We IMAGINE what it's like by experiencing it with our senses, our neurology to gain a new perspective. The more we practice this, the more we become what we are practicing just like anything else whether it's happiness or frustration we'll get good at what we practice.

We can choose greater lives and outcomes for ourselves, but we are going to need to explore and IMAGINE more extraordinary lives and opportunities to get there.

We will also need to address where our negative imagination takes us and heal it at its roots so we can be the ones creating our worlds, not our rerun buttons.

"When I let go of what I am, I become what I might be."
            -Lao Tzu

~ ~ ~ ~ I invite you to now explore the power of your IMAGINATION. ~ ~ ~ ~

Imagine there's a large plump, bright, juicy lemon fresh from the fridge covered in condensation just in front of you on a cutting board.

As you look to the side, you may notice a cutting knife. Take the knife and slice the lemon in half and as you do the lemon squirts its juices out at you as it fills the air with that fresh lemon aroma; it's almost as if you can already taste it's acidic super sour lemony taste.

As the lemon seeps onto the cutting board, you pick up the cold, waxy lemon as its juices soak your hand; you tilt your head back and squeeze all of the tart juice from the lemon onto your tongue. As you saturate your tongue with the sour tart tingling taste of the sharp, pungent lemon, you can feel your mouth pucker up as you salivate from that tart, tingly acidic taste of the lemon.

Now notice how juicy your mouth is, as you salivated preparing for the sour taste of the lemon.

All you had to do was IMAGINE a lemon to get an automatic, involuntary response from your body as it salivated preparing your tongue for the lemon; this is how Hypnosis works!

By using the power of your *IMAGINATION*, you can create very real change within your mind, body and soul.

Our breath is an automatic function, yet it is the one automatic function we can consciously control and when we do this conscious breathing it sends a powerful message to our subconscious.

As we slow our breath down and allow our conscious minds to relax and actively engage in trance, we can use our imagination to create powerful suggestions to take root within our subconscious mind.

It is through actively engaging our imaginations via hypnosis, self-hypnosis, meditation, NLP and daydreaming that we can sculpt our realities.

One of the best examples of the power of our imagination is demonstrated beautifully by none other than one of my favorite inventors, Nikola Tesla.

Tesla was a master of his mind and used his imagination to create and engage with his inventions. He never had to take notes and sketch things out but could trust all his work to be calculated to the finest of detail all within his mind.

Author, M.H Wisehart wrote an article in America magazine interviewing Tesla entitled:

"Making your imagination work for you."

Here's what Tesla said in the article.

"I found I could visualize with the greatest facility. I needed no models, drawings, or experiments. I could picture them all in my head."

"Here, in brief, is my own method: After experiencing a desire to invent a particular thing, I may go on for months or years with the idea in the back of my head. Whenever I feel like it, I'd roam around in my imagination and think about the problem without any deliberate concentration. This is a period of incubation."

"There follows a period of direct effort. I choose carefully the possible solutions of the problem I am considering, and gradually center my mind on a narrowed field of investigation. Now, when I am deliberately thinking of the problem in its specific features, I may begin to feel that I am going to get the solution. And the wonderful thing is that if I do feel this way, then I know I have really solved the problem and shall get what I am after."

"The feeling is as convincing to me as though I already had solved it. I have come to the conclusion that at this stage the actual solution is in my mind subconsciously though it may be a long time before I am aware of it consciously."

"Before I put a sketch on paper, the whole idea is worked out mentally. In my mind I change the construction, make improvements, and even operate the device. Without ever having drawn a sketch I can give the measurements of all parts to workmen, and when completed all these parts will fit, just as certainly as though I had made the actual drawings. It is immaterial to me whether I run my machine in my mind or test it in my shop."

"The inventions I have conceived in this way have always worked. In 30 years there has not been a single exception. My first electric motor, the vacuum tube wireless light, my turbine engine and many other devices have all been developed in exactly this way."

 Tesla was an incredible mind to say the least and as for his use of his powerful imagination, I believe he was really an expert in self-hypnosis, perhaps the very best.

 After years of practice, he was able to fine tune the art of seeking, listening, trusting and allowing the subconscious and SUPERCONSCIOUS to guide him and unfold the way.

Tesla is a brilliant mind to model and thankfully we are gifted with these deep insights on how he did his incredible work!

"The gift of mental power comes from God, Divine Being, and if we can concentrate our minds on that truth, we become in tune with great power."
~Nikola Tesla

CHAPTER 14
SEXY MAGNETIC YOU!

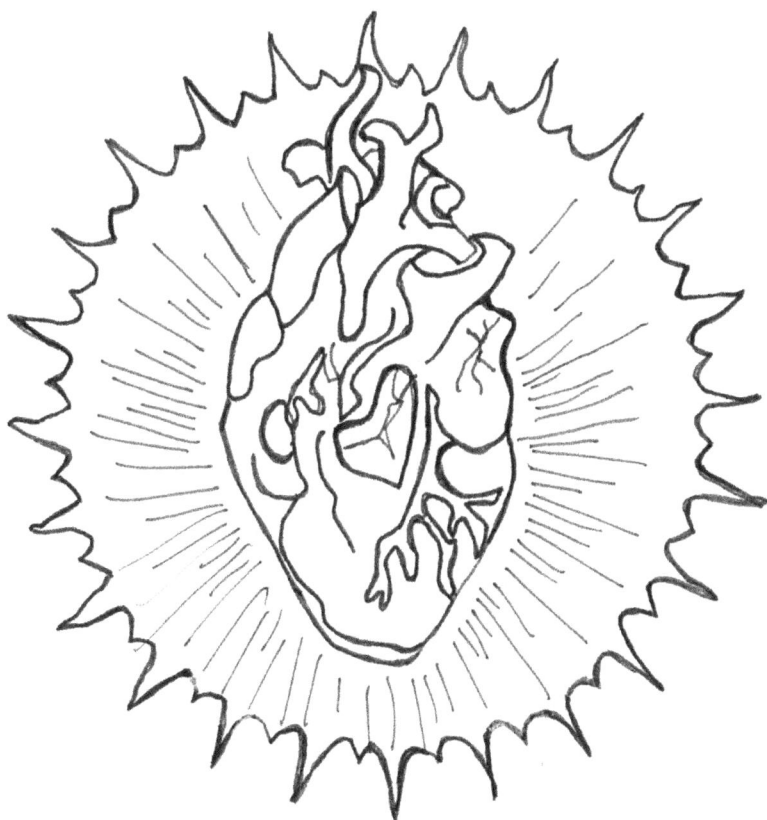

I know, I know.... Sexy Magnetic YOU!

Let's get to the spice already!

I'm sure you realize by now it's all about the spice and how you use it.

Yes, let's talk about SEXY MAGNETIC YOU!

What comes to mind when you think about Sexy Magnetic YOU?

What do you hear yourself saying in response? How do you deny it? How do you *CELEBRATE* it?

What do you envision, feel, or sense in whatever way that is important to you, in response?

If you could be exactly the kind of person that you truly, deeply want to be, what would you change to be that, Sexy Magnetic YOU?

~~ *YOU ARE THE ONE AND ONLY YOU!* ~~

There are no identical fingerprints for a reason and that's because we are all the very first and last one of our kind, when we own our unique identity.

If we were the first or last of a species, you bet we'd all be incredibly eager to honor, protect and explore this precious and unique one of a kind being.

YOU ARE A PRECIOUS* AND UNIQUE* ONE OF A KIND* BEING, and since you are the only you, you owe it to yourself and the rest of us to sincerely know, honor and love yourself just as you would an endangered species.

If we don't wake up to the truth of our unique identity, we will miss out on sharing our gifts and our unique purpose for being. If we do not own our unique identity, it will be forever lost like the species we are losing because we as the human race are out of balance in regards to our values and purpose. Why would we value the planet and its animal kingdom if we don't value ourselves?

When we embrace ourselves and allow the greatness within us to shine we are a sounding call for others to do the same. It is time for us to choose our most desired potentials and outcomes and commit to them so we can RISE and share more power, energy, clarity and inspiration, so we can tackle the big issues we all face together on this planet.

The truth is we NEED *Sexy Magnetic YOU!*

We NEED every single one of you because you have the only YOU to share with the rest of us.

You deserve to be the YOU; you genuinely want to be, sincerely happy and sharing your gifts unashamedly.

So yes, let's explore the treasure that is, Sexy Magnetic YOU!

What motivates you? What makes you tick? What thrills you to no end? What do you dream for yourself and the world around you? What excites you and brings you the deepest sense of JOY? What ignites you to go out there and make things happen? What drives you to go above and beyond? What do you value most about yourself and your environment and why? What is your PURPOSE?

Tesla was so aligned with his purpose that he was able to go above and beyond reasonable expectations and abilities because he knew his why?

"The desire that guides me in all I do is the desire to harness the forces of nature to the service of mankind."

~Nikola Tesla

Notice he said the **SERVICE** of mankind (humankind). When we are connected to our unique identities, we instinctively know deep down that we are here to **HELP**; this is why it is so important to connect within and find our answers, our gems within us that make us **SHINE** the way only we can!

When we know our PURPOSE, our WHY, this is pure ROCKET FUEL!

We've been conditioned to seek and value other people's dreams for us, including the media's dreams for us. True happiness and fulfillment live within honoring our inner truth. It is so important to take the time to answer as clearly and vividly as possible what YOUR DREAM or VISION is for YOUR LIFE?

What is YOUR STORY?

If you are the author and can erase the character others have told you to be, how would you tell your story? What would be different and why? If you could, what would you do? WHAT STOPS YOU?

It is so important to get unwaveringly clear on what your pure crystal-clear intention wants to create for your life and to work with someone who will hold you ACCOUNTABLE to your word.

Whether it's a coach or a friend you commit to being accountability partners with, we all need support if we want to grow because it's easier for someone else to see what we haven't yet seen because we ALL have blind spots.

Knowledge is power, and if someone is watching and holding us accountable, we will always raise our standards to be more and more of the person we genuinely want to be.

Knowing ourselves, and all of our strengths and weaknesses gives us the advantage because we can work on what challenges us until it's no longer a challenge and we can gracefully move on to more exciting challenges. If we are not aware of our talents and our blind spots, we can't explore and improve them.

You have an *infinite sea of greatness seeded within you* just waiting to be nurtured and explored, and all it takes to start the journey is to say yes to it, yes to **YOU!**

Just as every ripple in the sea creates the vastness of the ocean, your greatness affects everyone around you and can help inspire others to begin to explore their unique gifts and share them with the rest of us!

Imagine what our world would look like if we authentically loved and believed in ourselves and each other; honoring each other's GEMS; embracing ourselves and each other for our unique gifts we have to share with one another.

Just imagine if Martin Luther King, Rosa Parks, Gandhi or Mother Teresa decided to let self- doubt stop them from sharing their powerful unique destiny with our world.

Each one of them made a decision to follow through on their unique identity and chose to be a force of healing and we are forever grateful for their gifts to our humanity.

When we take the time to heal and honor the amazement that lives within each and every one of us, we are igniting a healing spark for the rest of the world to STAND UP to its potential. Ending the wars within us and around us and celebrating happiness and peace is the best first steps for creating the answers we need to create harmony and to begin to explore our true gifts of humanity.

Ok, back to SEXY!

SEXY.... what does that mean to you?

When do you feel sexy?

When you notice someone who's got sex appeal, what is it that appeals to you?

Of course, there are Hollywood conditioned perfectly geometrically aligned faces and bodies that can turn up the sizzle more than others but all that perfect body or face has to do is say something super off-putting to sink that erotic ship and fast!

As much as we've been conditioned to fall for the surface affair it's what's on the inside that keeps an attraction *ALIVE.*

There is nothing, and I mean nothing that can trump in sex appeal more than confidence. Not the cocky, needing to prove something kind; which is major turn-off material.

I'm talking about true confidence when you see someone who shines in the skin they're in. Especially when they are shining their unique identity, this exudes a charm and magnetism like nothing else.

When we feel good about ourselves, this rubs off on those around us making others feel good in our presence; the same is true for when we have a dark cloud above us, this too affects those around us; acting as a repellent.

SEXY MAGNETIC YOU! - is about owning your magnetism; owning yourself and your life and falling in love with your LIFE.

When you fill your own cup up with LOVE, you have something extremely valuable to bring to the table; this, in turn, creates the magnetism for others who too love themselves unconditionally and this is where the most fulfilling "sizzle" lives; by staying wide awake at the wheel of LIFE.

Alchemy begins when we dedicate ourselves to the never ending process of self-love, growth and discovery. When we encourage and INSPIRE growth from one another while holding the truth that it is our responsibility to keep awake at the wheel of life and all its wonder, we keep our awareness ALIVE and our ~A~ game *on*.

When we expect ourselves to be the seed that IS complete, as it grows and unfolds trusting and honoring ourselves and our magnetism by taking ownership of our lessons, this feeds a sense of hope and expansion to our environment inviting new and exciting possibilities.

When we care for ourselves, caring for our minds, bodies and our spirits, we are *IRRESISTIBLE!*

I don't care who you are, there is a perfect someone out there for you, and you are their perfect someone and the more you cultivate that feeling that you are that perfect someone and honor yourself and enjoy being that perfect someone the sooner that perfect fulfilling partner will manifest.

Again you have to believe into this; after all, what you believe = you achieve.

What would be different if you had said, perfect partner?

What would change?
What would change about you?

When you step into this dream/goal and vivify it, you can begin to create the perfect environment for its magnetism to find you. And this doesn't just have to be a romantic partner, it could be a work situation, friend or whatever it is you truly seek.

Would you spice up your wardrobe? Focus on being healthy and fit? Would it motivate you to improve your finances to begin a family or pursue other dreams and ambitions?

Waiting is a losing game, get clear on what your dream is for your life and what happiness looks like for you and

>>> GO FOR IT!

There's nothing sexier than someone who knows what they want and goes out and gets it.

Let's not forget about sexuality? Again there is no need to wait for a perfect partner to begin to feel safe, comfortable and extremely sexy within our sensuality and sexuality. Get in touch with yourself! There's a lot of pleasure to be found and explored, and you can celebrate your sensuality and sexuality anytime you choose! No need to wait to feel alive and empowered in your root chakra.

When we fulfill ourselves and are comfortable with receiving pleasure, this affects our health, happiness, and general well-being as well as is extremely sexy and exciting for our lovers when they see the enjoyment we are open to sharing.

There's no shame in enjoying our bodies and celebrating our sensual sexuality.

When we love the skin we are in and do our work regarding healing our internal blocks and taking action to create our lives to the utmost fulfillment this is as SEXY! As Sexy can be!

Happiness is SEXY!

Caring for our bodies by exercising, eating consciously and dressing to impress ourselves and the rest of the world is SEXY!

- Sexy is being PRESENT in this present moment.

- Sexy is being HONEST and TRUE.

- Sexy is taking responsibility for being the very best YOU!

- Sexy is being there for your fellow human being, and to be there for your fellow human being, you must first and foremost be present for yourself honoring your needs, creating clear boundaries and going full force towards your goals and dreams.

- Sexy is...

  >>>>>>>>*Sexy-Magnetic-YOU!*<<<<<<<<

- Sexy is not giving up on yourself.

- Sexy is daring to love yourself completely down to every single cell.

- Sexy is stretching beyond your comfort zone.

- Sexy is humility to grow in the face of challenge.

- Sexy is allowing yourself to be vulnerable.

- Sexy is saying YES! ... to YOU!

- Sexy is saying yes you are WORTHY!

- Sexy is COMMITTING TO LOVE!

- Sexy is, owning it all, the good, bad and the ugly for GOOD, not evil.

- Sexy is transforming the can't/s into CAN/S!

- Sexy is laughter, humor, and FUN!

- Sexy is comfortable in the stillness and silence.

- Sexy is AWAKE at the wheel of life, love and happiness.

- Sexy is creative, entertaining and curious.

- Sexy is you after a BIG Beautiful CRY.

- Sexy is you not standing for things that don't serve your highest good!

- Sexy is being at PEACE with yourself.

- Sexy is being OPEN TO DEEP CONNECTION because you have the courage to explore your own depths and in doing so gives you the ability to dive DEEP!

- Sexy is listening with an OPEN HEART to yourself and others and sharing from an honest place.

- Sexy is allowing the flame of your HEART to grow in its passion, depth and spark!*

- Sexy is believing in YOURSELF and saying I DO! -to yourself and life, through thick or thin.

- Sexy is those eyes in the mirror who believe in YOU!

- Sexy is SEXY MAGNETIC *YOU!!!*

BE TRUE to YOURSELF!

You are and will *always be...*

SEXY MAGNETIC YOU!

BELIEVE IN YOURSELF

&

SHINE

BRIGHTLY!

Exercise:

Write a love letter to Sexy Magnetic YOU,

Dearest (your name),

Now write a true blue love letter to yourself. The kind of love letter you have always wanted to receive and *mean it.* Open your heart to yourself and send love to all parts of you. Take the same time and care you would writing a love letter to the most incredible love of your life... because YOU ARE!
Send this letter with a stamped -self-addressed envelope so I can send this letter to you when you least expect it.

Mail to:
Sexy Magnetic You
Co/Vanessa Smith
P.O Box 40517
Austin Texas, 78704

It all begins NOW... not tomorrow... not next week... but NOW, at this very moment. If you don't do it now you will likely never do it so,

TAKE ~ACTION ~NOW!

- write the words you need and deserve to hear.

This is IMPORTANT, FOLLOW THROUGH!!! YOUR FUTUR- SELF WILL THANK YOU!

READY, SET, GO!

- And if you aren't up for sending a letter ...

Please just write one right here at the end of this book so every time you need a reminder you can simply pick it up and dive into those words that you need and deserve to hear! Frankly, I suggest you do both!

Write something beautiful you need to hear right here, right *now,* as well as <u>send a letter</u>, both will be *extremely therapeutic!*

Either way, I hope you choose to LOVE every cell in your mind, body and soul down to the DNA.

DEAREST SEXY MAGNETIC YOU,